WALKING
with
ANGELS

My 17 Personal Encounters with God and His Angels

Jeff Bentley

ISBN 979-8-88540-878-3 (paperback)
ISBN 979-8-88540-879-0 (digital)

Copyright © 2023 by Jeff Bentley

All rights reserved. No part of this publication may be reproduced, distributed, or transmitted in any form or by any means, including photocopying, recording, or other electronic or mechanical methods without the prior written permission of the publisher. For permission requests, solicit the publisher via the address below.

Christian Faith Publishing
832 Park Avenue
Meadville, PA 16335
www.christianfaithpublishing.com

Printed in the United States of America

Dedication

To John Bates.

    As I began my morning walk in July, my phone rang, and it was a longtime dear friend of mine, Cindy. We took a few moments to briefly catch up on life and family. After raising four daughters, she and her husband, Bates, finally had their first grandson in the family. His name is John Bates. She was beyond excited. Cindy posed a special request of me. Cindy asked me to put together something that she could give to young John as he grew up that would help him in some way. It could be a word, a phrase, a paragraph, or just anything that I felt would make a positive impact on a young man growing up in this tough world we live in. It was an honor to receive such a request and a responsibility that I took very seriously. I told her I most certainly would and began to pray asking the Lord for direction on what advice and wisdom I should provide this young man.

    The Lord led me to a time of reflection. Looking back over my life at all of the events and special times where I inquired upon the Lord for direction, for help, and, of course, His will, the only advice and wisdom I could give anyone is from my own "faith" experiences. For instance, my wife, Juli, and I had raised three boys, and they are all grown now. As I reflected back on some of the advice I gave my sons, I couldn't help but recall the one thing I told them repeatedly. That was "I'm the one that loves you and cares about you more than anyone in this world. I have been where you are going. If I can ever help you or answer any questions along the way, please ask me. I will *always* be there for you."

I had a sizable head start on life and didn't want them making the same mistakes I had made. I wanted them to benefit from the things I had learned and be prepared for the challenges that life brings. I wanted them to know they could always pick up the phone and call their father for absolutely anything.

After a month and a half of prayerful consideration, I notified Cindy that I knew what I was going to do and I would be in touch. I began to write about the personal experiences that I had since childhood that emphatically involved the Lord and His angels.

The following "faith" experiences are very real. By the time I had finished, they had become my personal testimony as well as the Lord's testimony of what He's done in my life.

I pray that you will learn from my fifty-five-year head start in life and benefit from a blessed life way before I did. I want you to know that all you have to do is seek Him and call on the Father!

Contents

Acknowledgments vii
Introduction ix

1: Comfort During Times of Grief—Divorce, Moving, and Sister Passes Away 1
2: Peace Knowing God Was in Control—a Loving Christian Wife 6
3: Protection When I Needed It the Most—Saved From Certain Death While Digging Fence Postholes 11
4: Provision of a New Job as My Company Files Bankruptcy 15
5: Living on Faith—Changing Industries and Receiving Provision by Serving Others 20
6: Vision "Go Build My Kingdom" Is Given to Me 26
7: Provision and Confirmation—Firsthand Experience of Building on Faith with Habitat for Humanity 31
8: Guidance upon Request as I Searched for My Ancestor's Grave 36
9: Protected Again from Serious Injury while Driving at Night 41
10: Provision, Guidance, and Blessing during Weekly Prayer Calls 45
11: Guidance, Protection, and Gratitude as I'm Directed to the Emergency Room 49
12: Affirmation and Blessings after Taking God Up on His Promise 55

13: Healing during a Time of Recovery	60
14: Rescued from Dark Times by an Angel	69
15: The Finger of God—the Lord's Testimony of Provision	74
16: Revelation as "Build My Kingdom" Is Given to Me in Great Detail	77
17: Confirmation of an Angel's Presence upon Request	82
My Deepest Regret	91
It Is My Hope	95

Acknowledgments

I want to give a special thanks to Os Hillman for feeding me God's word every single day over the last fifteen years. Os and his wife, Pamela, produce the online daily devotional Today God Is First (TGIF) along with Marketplace Leaders—Helping You Fulfill God's Calling. Not only do I get to read God's word every day, I get a real life application from Os that shows me how to apply each verse to my life. The spiritual encouragement that I have received from this devotional and the emphasis on fulfilling one's calling has everything to do with my personal testimony. If it weren't for his daily devotionals hitting my inbox every morning, I'm not so sure I would be here today.

I can't express my sincere thanks and gratitude enough to Os for blessing my life over the years and allowing the Lord to speak through him. He has a true gift from God. His influence on my spiritual journey can be seen in every chapter of this book.

www.TodayGodIsFirst.com

Introduction

I was just a normal kid that grew up in a family living in a suburb north of Dallas. I experienced everything that most people experience growing up—divorce, death, moving, playing sports, college, marriage, raising kids, challenges in business, and times wandering away from God. I didn't grow up "in" the church. I grew up visiting the church on a semi-frequent basis. I didn't have an intimate relationship with Christ at all. I was the kid that was afraid to pray in front of others. I accepted Jesus as my Lord and Savior when I was fifteen years old. I became a deacon in the church in my hometown. I have no formal training or education in theology and certainly no training as a writer. So why am I writing this? Because I was blessed to receive a special request from my friend Cindy. After much prayerful consideration, I have been led by the Holy Spirit to bring forth something we all want to see—proof that God exists on a personal level. I can emphatically say He most certainly does! He's not a distant figure that we read about in the Bible. He's available practically "on demand." The truth is encouraging and sometimes painful to write. The only credentials that I have are firsthand encounters with God, His angels, and a little nudge from Leslie in our church bookstore to write it all down here.

Being the independent one that I am, I've taken my own path, and that has provided me my share of challenges. Consequently, my learning has been based upon my experiences rather than my reading. I love adventure, and looking back over the last sixty-one years, my life has certainly been an adventure. At this point in my life, reflecting back on some of my adventures was something that I would never have done if it weren't for my friend Cindy. It never occurred to me that my life was any different than anyone else's life. Maybe it isn't, I don't know. But when telling others about my past experiences leads to the question "Are you going to write a book?" I've learned that's God's way of speaking to us. I am certainly not an English major, and writing was never my strongest suit. What is contained in the following pages are heartfelt accounts of what has happened in my life. They are very personal. I'm now convinced that others besides John Bates should hear what the Lord has done in my life. This is a first for me. Any grace while reading these accounts is much appreciated.

In the following pages, I have put together the Lord's testimony along with my personal testimony on what He and His angels have done in my life. This is by all means not everything, they are the highlights of my life. Testimony comes from the Hebrew word *eduwth*, which means "witness." I am your witness to the power of what God can do in a person's life. I learned along the way that as long as I continued to seek His will in my life, He would bless me and my journey to discover my purpose and His plans for me. He would then allow me the opportunity to carry out His will as long as I followed Him.

My purpose is to provide insight and a great deal of encouragement, inspiration, and uplifting to just how awesome God really is. Over the course of my life, I've had many occasions where the Lord answered my prayers immediately. Many of those answered prayers changed my life. I want you to know that He will guide you and protect you as you go through life. He's done that for me.

What I'm about to share with you are some seemingly ordinary and some extraordinary interactions with God. At this moment, I can recall seventeen very memorable encounters with God and His angels. I want to share those experiences with you so that you can tell everyone you know that God and His angels are real and they are with us every day. As a result of these encounters, I've experienced these things:

- Comfort during times of grief
- Peace and provision knowing that God was in control
- Provision when I needed it
- Protection such as saving my life—multiple times
- Gratitude for watching over me
- Guidance when I needed it
- Vision on His plans for me
- Blessings when I least expected them
- Affirmation that kept me going
- Healing when my body needed it
- Being rescued during a dark time in my life
- God's testimony of provision
- Confirmation to let me know He is always there
- Revelation so I may carry out His plans in my life

Some of these encounters were direct answers to prayer, and I knew immediately that God was present. Other times, God used his angels to directly intervene in my life, causing me to act in a way that wound up saving my life. Angels literally saved my life on four separate occasions. At the time, some seemed like coincidences, and each time left me in total amazement as to what had just happened.

It wasn't until years later the I looked back and realized that none of those instances were coincidence, chance, or luck. They were the hand of God protecting me and guiding me. Now that I'm more aware, I watch for it every day. I'm much more attentive to what goes on in my life.

You may be wondering how I know that it's God and His angels that are doing this. The scriptures tell all of us about God and His angels protecting us and guiding us.

Psalm 91:11–14 NIV states,

> For He will command His angels concerning you to guard you in all your ways. 'I will protect him for he acknowledges my name.'

There's no doubt God and His angels protected and guided me. I want to encourage you to know that the Lord, along with His angels, will protect and guide you too!

1

Comfort During Times of Grief—Divorce, Moving, and Sister Passes Away

It was December of 1968, and my sister Jill and I were in my bedroom playing, and my mom walked into the room and shut the door. She asked us to sit up on the bed. She wanted to tell us something. She began to explain that although she and Dad loved us very much, we were no longer going to live together as a family. They had decided to get a divorce. At eight years old, the concept of what a divorce was and what it meant was extremely foreign to me. My little sister was only three years old, too young to understand what was said and continued to play in my room. I began to ask many questions. The first question was "Why?" My mom gently consoled me by saying that she would have to tell me later. It would be much later—once I was old enough to understand. Mom began to explain that the three of us would be moving and I would be going to a different school and get to make new friends. Just like any young child, I didn't want to break up our family, I didn't want to leave my dad, I didn't want to move, I didn't want to change schools, and I wasn't interested in making new friends. I just wanted everything to stay the same and be okay.

The coming days would be very traumatic for me and my little sister. My dad just disappeared. He didn't come to us and explain what was going on. He didn't tell us that he still loved us and that we would be seeing him again. Nothing. It would be twenty-eight years before my dad told me anything. That's when it occurred to me. We stopped seeing him the moment he stopped making child support payments to my mom. For him, the financial obligation was more important than the love for his two children.

Sometime later, my mom then introduced my sister and I to this new man in her life, and they decided to get married after a few short months of dating. We moved into a new home, and I began the third grade in a new school. I missed my old life. I missed growing up in the house that my granddad built. I missed living across the street from my cousins and around the corner from my grandparents. I missed going to my other grandparents' farm out in the country where I got to fish and shoot my BB gun. I missed driving the pasture in the back of my granddad's truck as he checked on his herd of Hereford cattle. And I most certainly missed sitting on the tailgate of his truck on the opening day of dove season as all of my uncles and cousins gathered in that yearly ritual of coming together. It was hard, and it hurt. A lot. My grandparents' farm is now a golf course. There's only one tree left where their farmhouse once was. I sometimes hop the fence and go stand next to that tree and reflect on all the wonderful times I had there. It's something that I miss to this very day.

After a few months, we seemed to settle into our new lives, living in a new neighborhood and making new friends. There were no more nasty arguments at the dinner table, no more objects being thrown across the room, and no more seeing my mom cry like I did before. Life seemed to be getting better living with my new dad.

By now it was January 26, 1971, a Sunday evening, and I was playing at my friend Charlie's house down the street. I was ten years old at the time, and I was told to be home by sundown. As I was walking down the sidewalk just as the sun was setting, I heard sirens in the distance. As I arrived at my house, an ambulance pulled up in front of our house. I then turned to see my dad carrying my little sister out to meet the paramedics in our driveway. Jill was unconscious as they laid her down on the stretcher right in front of me. I had no idea what had happened, and there wasn't time for an explanation. They quickly whisked her and my mom off to the hospital in the ambulance. My dad followed them to the hospital in his car, and I was left standing on the driveway with my friend, Charlie, and his mom. Charlie's mom had agreed to watch me over the next few days while my sister was in the hospital.

Over the next couple of days, I was allowed to go to the hospital to see my sister lying there unconscious with all the tubes in her. I was told she had an aneurysm in her brain, and that was the last time I saw her alive. She passed away the next day and went to be with Jesus.

As our family grieved over the loss of my little sister, it was during that time that I was taught to pray and ask God to heal our family and comfort us during that time.

A few months passed by, and my parents told me they were expecting a child. The child's expected delivery date was the upcoming January. My new baby brother, Brian, was born on January 26, 1972. Exactly one year to the day my little sister got into that ambulance and never came home again. Over the next several years, it dawned on me that my new little brother was born exactly one year later, and I thought that was a quite a coincidence for something like that to happen. As I grew closer to the Lord and better understood how he communicates with us, I have come to realize that God was in control all along. That's when God showed up on my radar. It was just a simple way for Him to let a small eleven-year-old boy know that He had a better plan.

Many years later, my mom told me that something told her to get me and my sister out of that horrible living arrangement we were in. It was a mother's intuition. Her spirit was most certainly guided by the Holy Spirit to a safer place to raise her two kids. The Lord directed her steps and guided her path. We were provided a new home to live in with a wonderful man that raised us and earned the name of "Dad." Although life was very different with my new dad, we were protected and blessed by the Lord during those tough times.

Looking back

They say that hindsight is twenty-twenty, and time heals all wounds. I suppose much of that is true. At the time of those events, the emotions were raw, and the uncertainty was high. When I stand back and look at what took place nearly fifty years ago, I can see the hand of God at work. The Holy Spirit spoke to my mom's spirit and guided all of us out of a bad situation. He provided my mom a loving, caring man that loved me and my sister. Even though we had to move and start all over, it turned out to be a blessing. At the time, I was too young to pick up on the big picture and see God's hand guiding and protecting us. When my sister passed away, it left us all grieving and wondering where God was. He was there all along. He was in control, and He proved that by blessing my mom and dad with a new son born exactly one year later.

I learned that no matter if you are young in age or a young Christian, God is always in control whether you realize it or not. He never left us, and He gave us comfort. Having a front-row seat at being a witness was my first "faith experience" that began to shape my walk with the Lord.

The following verses gave us comfort and peace during those times:

> Those who sow in tears will reap with songs of joy. (Psalm 126:5 NIV)
>
> For the Lord your God goes with you; he will never leave you nor forsake you. (Deuteronomy 31:6 NIV)
>
> He heals the broken hearted and binds up their wounds. (Psalm 147:3 NIV)
>
> Now faith is being sure of what we hope for and certain of what we do not see. (Hebrews 11:1 NIV)

The Lord replied,

> My child, I would never leave you. During your times of trial, when you see only one set of footprints, it was then that I carried you. (Author unknown)

2

Peace Knowing God Was in Control—a Loving Christian Wife

I was attending college in Austin and had been dating several girls, and I increasingly became frustrated that none of the girls I had been dating were anything close to what I would consider marriage material. As a matter of fact, the more girls I dated, the more frustrated I got. Taking a date to a movie was a lost opportunity to get to know them. Now please understand, I was not actively looking for a wife, but I was hoping to find a meaningful relationship with a Christian girl to spend time with. That's nothing new—practically every man experiences this during his younger days. I was attending the largest college in the Southwestern United States with more than 50,000 students. Surely, I could find one Christian girl that I was compatible with. After three years at college, I dated quite a few girls, but none that I would consider meaningful. So I began to pray, asking God to provide me with a loving Christian girl of His choosing, not mine.

After high school, I had been introduced to a beautiful girl from back home while playing summer league baseball. Her name was Tina. I was smitten and wanted that relationship to work so badly. The more I got to know Tina, the more I liked her. We dated on and off during our first three years of college, but Tina liked to play games with the guys she dated. Her physical beauty was striking, and she knew it. She was used to getting her way, but so was I. I didn't fall for her little games. Dating Tina was an emotional roller coaster. The good times were great, and the not-so-good times were extremely frustrating. I began to see red flags in our relationship that I didn't want any part of. I continued to ask God to give me direction, and the last thing I wanted to do was continue in a relationship that wouldn't work for either person. After much continued prayer, I decided to stop seeing Tina. It was difficult to walk away from that relationship, but that's where the Holy Spirit was leading me.

During my senior year, I moved back home to finish college at UTD. I was taking classes at odd hours, and once my grandfather and my uncle found out that I was home and available, he asked me to assist him as he was building a large addition on to the Allen National Bank. After a few weeks working on the exterior of the building, we moved into the interior and began finishing out the rooms that we were adding. Since the bank opened at 8:30 every morning, we would arrive and begin working at 7:30 to do as much work as possible before the bank opened.

On one particular Monday morning, I was given two simple tasks to complete before lunchtime that day. I had to paint two exterior doors on the back side of the bank. One door was to be painted dark brown, and the other door was to be painted a light beige. As I began to mask off the wall around the first door that I was supposed to paint dark brown, I noticed a new bank employee that started her first day on the job as a bank secretary. Her desk was next to Bobbi's desk. Bobbi was the secretary to the president of the bank (the president of the bank just happened to be my uncle Dan). I had known Bobbi for some time, and she was like part of the family. The door I was about to paint was directly in front of Bobbi's desk. As I watched this new bank employee walk in and out of the room, I quietly asked Bobbi, "Who is that new girl?"

Bobbi immediately began to laugh out loud and whispered to me, "She just asked the same question about you!" Did I mention that this new girl was drop-dead gorgeous? Well, needless to say, that little episode got me all flustered, and I wound up painting that door the wrong color. That's right—I painted it light beige!

It took me a really long time to paint that first door, so by 10:30 a.m., I moved over to the other side of the bank to paint the other door. By now, everyone in the bank had learned of the "incident" and wrongly painted door in front of Bobbi's desk! My uncle Henry, the carpenter, suddenly placed his face upon the glass as I was painting the exterior of the other door. I stepped back, and he opened the door. He pushed the new gorgeous bank employee out through the door and said, "This is Juli, and she doesn't have anyone to take her to lunch today!" and then shut the door and left us alone outside. I immediately asked Juli if we could go to lunch that day, and she said yes. We went to lunch that day, Tuesday, Wednesday, Thursday, and Friday. We went out on our first date that Friday night, another date on Saturday night, and I spent all Sunday afternoon with her. We went to lunch every day after that and went out on dates every weekend from then on.

It truly was love at first sight. After knowing and dating Juli for only three months, I asked her to marry me. We were married exactly one year later from the day we met. Juli and I have three grown sons, Brandon, Cameron, and Wesley, and have been married for thirty-eight years. She is the love of my life and my best friend. We say "I love you" before we hang up on every phone call and anytime we depart from each other's company. We don't take each other for granted. We have been blessed by the Lord, and we know it!

March 3, 2022—thirty-eighth wedding anniversary

Looking back

What I learned from dating was I needed to experience what works and what doesn't work in a relationship. The earlier I learned about important issues like faith, core values, and compatibility, the easier it got. Time seems to reveal what doesn't work. The red flags go up and then we grew apart from one another. The more I experienced that, the better I got at it. A broken heart is painful, and I either had to learn from it or avoid the potential for it to reoccur. I chose the former and learned from those experiences and found myself to a point where I knew what I wanted and what I didn't want in a meaningful relationship. I knew that I would recognize genuine heartfelt love when I saw it. Dating countless girls seemed exhausting but necessary. That's a refining process I had to learn. I had to earn the right to be a good mate before God placed that person in my life.

Having been involved in a divorced family, I had made a personal commitment to myself that I would never get a divorce. I just wouldn't get married until I was sure it was the relationship that God intended for me.

After placing my dating life in God's hands and many attempts at finding the "right one," she appeared out of nowhere! Just when I least expected it. I never believed in love at first sight until then. Now I'm a firm believer.

Only God could have provided me with the perfect mate. That was an enormous answer to prayer and overwhelmingly affirmed to me that God has a specific person for each of us as long as we place it in His hands.

The following verses gave me peace during this time of my life:

> Take delight in the Lord and He will give you the desires of your heart. (Psalm 37:4 NIV)

> He who finds a wife finds what is good and receives favor from the Lord. (Proverbs 18:22 NIV)

> For the eyes of the Lord are on the righteous and His ears are attentive to their prayer. (1 Peter 3:12 NIV)

3

Protection When I Needed It the Most— Saved From Certain Death While Digging Fence Postholes

After our wedding in March 1984, we bought our first home in east Plano. It was not just any home. I actually built it while working as a construction superintendent for a local builder. It was a very nice small custom home on a large corner lot. In those days, the builders did not install sprinkler systems or fences in the backyard. So I decided that my first project was to install the sprinkler system. After several days of trenching, laying the pipes in the ground, and connecting the electrical, we finished the project. My second project was to install the wood fence in the backyard. I had decided to install the fence by myself. The first thing I needed to do was rent a gas-powered auger and drill the postholes for the fence posts. Here's a photo of a gas-powered auger similar to the one I used to drill the holes for my fence:

I had placed a piece of tape on the auger three feet from the tip so that I would know when I had gone deep enough for each posthole. I had all of the fence postholes dug except for one hole that was up next to the house near the electrical meter base. The meter base is where all the electricity comes into the house. It is run underground from the transformer behind our fence next to the alley. There are thousands of volts that run through those electrical lines from the transformer into my home. Enough voltage to kill an elephant. As I began to dig the last hole, I used extreme caution so I wouldn't hit the high-voltage power lines that are three feet deep. After digging halfway down, about one and a half feet, something told me to stop digging. I was nowhere near deep enough and was planning on digging to at least two and a half feet deep before stopping. After pulling the auger out of the hole, I reached down with my hand to grab a handful of loose dirt at the bottom of the hole. My hand immediately came into contact with the high-voltage power lines that were supposed to be three feet deep. One more turn of the auger blade would have scraped the insulated cover from the high-voltage power lines and killed me instantly!

The moment I reached down and felt the insulated cover of the braided three wires of those power lines, I got that sick feeling in my stomach. The familiar sick feeling when we sometimes receive dreadful news or when something bad has happened. It's an adrenaline rush that stops you in your tracks. Afterward, I immediately sat down on the ground next to that hole with the shakes.

I began to wonder why I decided to stop digging at one and a half feet deep when I was one foot away from my predetermined stopping point. There was no reason to stop when I did. At that moment, I knew it wasn't coincidence or luck. I knew immediately that someone was looking out for me. As I grew older and learned more about how God protects us, I can honestly say that I believe it was one of God's angels that caused me to stop digging at that moment, saving my life! He was protecting me because it was not my time.

Years later I was telling my kids the story of how I was miraculously spared from certain death by electrocution. My son Wesley asked, "Dad, how did you know to stop digging at that moment?"

My reply was simply, "An angel of the Lord caused me to stop!" Some things just can't be explained. That's when you know.

Looking back

When I was young, I thought I was bulletproof. I never thought of the risks, and I certainly didn't take precautions like I should have. All I had to do was call the 1-800-Dig line, and someone would have come out and marked the electrical line locations. Why would I do that? I thought I knew where the lines were. I did, but I didn't know how deep they were. My testosterone had overloaded my common sense. It wasn't the first or the last time that would happen. I'm amazed that I've lived this long considering some of the silly things I've done.

The event that took place that day in my backyard shook me to my core. It really rattled me. It was no different than being saved by an oncoming train. The only difference was there were no witnesses. Well, except for the angel that saved me.

What I learned that day was the Lord will send His angels and intervene if necessary. He did that because He loves me. He protected me even when I couldn't protect me from myself.

The following verses encouraged me of God's protection and my gratitude for Him:

> For He will command His angels concerning you to guard you in all your ways; they will lift you up in their hands, so that you will not strike your foot against a stone. (Psalm 91:11–12)

> Because he loves me," says the Lord, "I will rescue him; I will protect him, for he acknowledges my name. (Psalm 91:14)

> Praise Him, all His angels; praise Him, all His heavenly hosts. (Psalm 148:2)

4

Provision of a New Job as My Company Files Bankruptcy

It was October 1986, and I was head of construction for the eastern division of a local home building company. It was a Friday morning, and we let nine of our construction superintendents go that day. The real estate market and the oil industry were taking a dive in Texas, and it was finally hitting the DFW market. As the following weeks went by, I began to experience difficulties cashing my paychecks on Friday afternoons. My boss that I most admired had left the company a few months earlier, and I never inquired about his departure. Did he know something that I didn't? I was so young and naive I didn't recognize the signs. My wife was pregnant with our first child, and the baby was due in March. I had houses that needed to be completed and future homeowners that were depending on me to get their homes completed. I just figured that someone there could figure out this mess and turn things around.

One late afternoon as I was headed out the door to go to my car, the owner of the company stopped me. He said that I may want to start looking for another job because he wasn't sure how much longer he could keep the company going. I was shocked, to say the least. We had only been living in our new home the company built just a few years. My wife was about to take maternity leave, and now I was about to be unemployed! I began to pray that the Lord would find a solution to our dilemma. I didn't care what it was, where it was, or anything. I had a new baby that was sixty days away from being born. I needed a miracle!

The very next afternoon, I received a phone call from a home builder who was in town attending the national homebuilder's convention in Dallas. He was looking for a vice president of construction for his expanding home building company in Indianapolis, Indiana. He wanted to know if I could drive down to the Stouffer Hotel and meet him for an interview. I couldn't say yes fast enough, and off I went. We met for three hours, and he introduced me to the rest of his management team that evening. He wanted to offer me the job right then and there but said that wouldn't be fair. He said we need to come to Indianapolis and better understand the company, the people, the city, schools, churches, and especially the weather! Yes, he wanted me to see what the winter was like in January in the Midwest. So he booked Juli and I on a flight for the very next Friday evening. The night before the flight out, he called me and suggested that we may want to push our trip back one or two weeks due to the cold weather that had just pushed through the area. I appreciated the call, but I told him I needed to see the good and the bad of what Indianapolis had to offer.

On the flight up to Chicago, I prayed that whatever happened in the next few days, God would make it abundantly clear what we should do. I didn't have a lot of experience in these kind of situations, and I didn't want to mess this up. So we deplaned at Chicago's O'Hare Airport and had to walk down the ramp outside and walk into the terminal before boarding our next flight. The instant I took my first step on the ramp, the extreme cold took my breath away. It was negative two degrees in Chicago. We then boarded a short flight to Indianapolis where it had warmed up to zero degrees.

At the end of the weekend tour, the builder offered me the job making the same amount of money that Juli and I were making combined back in Texas. That would mean Juli would not have to get a job and would be able to stay home with our newborn baby. Wow! What a blessing! On the return flight home, Juli and I looked at each other and unanimously agreed that the opportunity that was placed before us was the best thing for our new family. The Lord blessed us with this out-of-nowhere opportunity!

We came home and informed my mom that we needed to put the house on the market for sale. She was a Realtor and was happy to help us. At that time, the housing market in the DFW area was on a downward slide. Property values were going down each month. It just so happened that one of my newly married classmates from high school came along just in the nick of time and bought our home. We netted a profit of $63 on the sale of our home. My mom told us that if our house would have taken one more month to sell, we would have lost a minimum of $10,000! Wow! What a blessing!

During the middle of trying to sell our home, my first son, Brandon, was born. It worked out that after he was about a month old, both Juli and Brandon were able to move up to Indy, and we would finally be together as a family.

We quickly found a church home of relocated Texans that made us feel right at home. Our other two sons were born there, and they loved growing up in the Midwest. The Lord was watching over us every step of the way and guided us to a smooth transition in Indianapolis where we lived happily for six years. We made lifelong friends there that we still love very much.

Looking back

The first thing I learned was, God is in the relocation business. He knew that my company was about to go under, and He knew that we wouldn't have the income to meet our financial obligations. Here's the great part—there was a wonderful Christian family that owned a home building business in Indianapolis, Indiana, that had been praying that the Lord would provide them the right person to fill their need in that company. As the Lord's will would have it, things worked out well for both parties. To this day, I have no idea how they found my name. That's how awesome He is! Just another day for God, but a life changer for our family!

I learned that God has unpredictable ways of carrying out His will. It became abundantly clear that my own abilities were not good enough, my network of people wasn't large enough, and my imagination to pull it all together wasn't creative enough. I had to learn to let it go and let God take control of our situation. That was extremely difficult for someone who was paid on their ability to control things. Daily prayer and time reading His word prepared me to do what I needed to do. I had to get out of my comfort zone and give up control. God showed me that His results work out perfectly.

The fact that God arranged for that call to be made was a testimony to the awesome power of God. I had done nothing to cause that to happen. He was glorified in that moment in my life! It was another incredible "faith experience" that strengthened my walk with Him!

The following verses encouraged me about God's provision:

> So do not fear, for I am with you; do not be dismayed, for I am your God. I will strengthen you and help you; I will uphold you with my righteous right hand. (Isaiah 41:10 NIV)

> And without faith it is impossible to please God, because anyone who comes to Him must believe that he exists and that He rewards those who earnestly seek Him. (Hebrews 11:6 NIV)

> I can do everything through Him who gives me strength. (Philippians 4:13 NIV)

5

Living on Faith—Changing Industries and Receiving Provision by Serving Others

It was August of 1992, and Hurricane Andrew had just hit the southern section of Florida. It was a massive category 5 hurricane that decimated the entire area. A major home builder in the area recruited me to come down and take over their operations. They were battling cost increases and construction delays due to high subcontractor turnover. A large majority of subcontractors were leaving their home builder work and heading to Homestead, Florida, to work for the insurance companies making three to four times the normal amount they could make working for home builders. This created massive problems for all of the home builders in the southern part of Florida. I remember driving up to the Orlando area just to look for a painter for our builders. Very soon after the hurricane, we were not able to finish our homes due to the subcontractor issues. Our hard costs were increasing daily due to these issues, and we had no idea what our houses would cost or when they'd be completed. The owner of our company shut our model homes down and stopped selling until the issue improved. That resulted in very significant downsizing, and I was forced to look at my other options.

My mom had always told me that I would make a good real estate professional. I never paid much attention to her for two reasons. One, I'd never sold a thing in my life up to that point, and didn't know the slightest thing about selling real estate. Two, that would mean a 100 percent commissioned income. I had been climbing the corporate ladder in the home building industry and was most comfortable with my high-paying salary and bonus income. Additionally, our third son had just been born, and the thought of making a living on 100 percent commission scared me to death. The day came when the downsizing affected me, and we moved back to Texas on the last day of December 1993.

The first business day of the new year found me sitting in real estate school, working to qualify for a real estate license while I lived with my parents. After a month of classes, I took the state exam and passed. I had to wait for my license to come in the mail, and on March 1, 1994, I started selling real estate with Re/Max Plano. I was absolutely terrified! My mom gave me the one-hour training that she promised, and I was suddenly pushed into the deep end. Here I was with three small children, a dedicated wife working full-time, taking care of everyone, while I was unemployed, every day attempting to do something I had no experience doing and no idea how to do it! Did I mention that I was terrified? Needless to say, I had been praying that the Lord would come through and help us land on our feet. However, this was not only a job change. This was an industry change, which meant I couldn't qualify for a home loan for at least two years.

These were the days before the internet, and so I spent as much time as possible doing "phone time." That's when prospective buyers and sellers would call our office, interested in buying a home or listing their current home, and our office had a dedicated group of Realtors ready to answer the phones and happily assist them. We worked in three-hour shifts, answering the phones and either assisting potential buyers and sellers or making showing appointments for other Realtors wanting to show our listings. I began to ask all of the senior Realtors in the office that had established businesses if I could take their phone shifts each month. I accumulated as many three-hour phone shifts as I could as I honed my craft, learning how to listen and serve others.

I eagerly watched every move my mom made with her real estate business and wanted my phone to ring just like hers did. She gave me two great pieces of advice. First, remember that you aren't selling anything. You are listening for the need and helping buyers find what they want in a home and helping sellers maximize their home sale. Second, she said to take care of every client just as if it were her I was working with. In other words, take care of them like family. Two of the best pieces of advice I've ever received. I put my head down and got to work. I put in many hours learning how to listen so that I would have the skill set in order to excel at serving others.

In the first seventeen days of phone time, the Lord blessed me with three home sales. I continued to put in the time, and I continued to be amazed at the results. God had definitely guided me and blessed our family during this very stressful time of my life. Yes, my mom gave me guidance and assisted me along the way, but it was the Lord that provided. The timing of His provision and how smoothly those first transactions went made me stand back in amazement. Apparently, I had a gift that only He knew. I had found my calling.

I was a kid that grew up in a family of home builders. I grew up with a hammer in my hand. The thought of someone in the construction side of the business moving over to the sales side of the business was unheard of. It just didn't happen. Those were two totally different skill sets. I was put in this situation where I had to lean on God and allow Him to do His work in me!

Looking back

Now this was a new "faith experience" with a twist. Not only did I find myself looking for a new job that included another cross-country move, but this time it required a totally different skill set that I didn't know I had. The stakes just kept getting higher. By now we had three sons all under the age of seven. I had a newly printed real estate license in my back pocket and had to learn on the job how to convert that to income. I sometimes referred to it as being "unemployed every day with a license to eat." Meaning we only eat if we close a home. Talk about getting out of one's comfort zone. I was receiving an indoctrination in the school of living on faith. I had to learn that faith is spelled r-i-s-k. I had to lean on the Lord to bring in new potential clients. I had to lean on the Lord to help me develop my new skill of listening. Then I had to learn how to assist my clients during the home buying/selling process to a successful closing. All of which I had absolutely no experience doing. I seemed to be doing quite a bit of leaning on the Lord during those early days of serving others. Honestly, it was nothing short of a miracle that I ever sold anything.

There have been numerous times where I received a call from a new buyer or a new seller that told me they prayed, asking the Lord to provide them a Realtor to assist them. Adding that they didn't know anyone, and after asking their close friends, they were referred to me. While I am praying that the Lord would provide me a new buyer or seller client, these future clients were praying for a trustworthy and competent Realtor! The Lord is definitely in the networking business too! This has happened on many occasions over the years, and every time it happens, it encourages me to continue blessing them and to make a difference is someone's life.

As I look back during those times, the Lord was preparing me by living on faith and allowing Him to provide all of the family's needs through this new vocation. He was preparing me to learn how to listen carefully and be more attentive to people and what was being said. And later, as the years in sales added up, He reminded me that my success had nothing to do with me. He owned my business, and He was allowing me to be a steward with the provisions that He provided. My job was to learn how to be obedient and give Him back his share. Unfortunately, that part wouldn't come until much later.

In 2 Kings 4:2, 7 it says that the servant had nothing but a little oil. The servant was told to go sell the oil and use the proceeds to live off of. I learned that my "oil" was my ability to serve others with their real estate needs.

I look back at that transition in my life twenty-eight years ago and am in awe of how God controlled every step of the way as He provided for our family. I love what I do and wouldn't consider anything else. I later learned that I'm the seventh generation in my family of real estate professionals going back to the Republic of Texas days before Texas became a state. I have a rich heritage in real estate that I am most honored to be a part of, and it's only by the grace of God that I was able to find my way.

My faith has grown exponentially during that period as the Lord has used me to bless others as they transition in life. One "faith experience" seems to build upon the next "faith experience." Being in survival mode much of the time, I was nowhere near smart enough to catch on to what God was doing in my life. Looking back, I can see His plan coming together.

The following verses encouraged me about God's plan and His provision:

> Each one should use whatever gift he has received to serve others, faithfully administering God's grace in its various forms. (1 Peter 4:10 NIV)

> Whatever you do, work at it with all your heart, as working for the Lord, not for men, since you know that you will receive an inheritance from the Lord as a reward. It is the Lord Christ you are serving. (Colossians 3:23–24 NIV)

> Your servant has nothing there at all, except a little oil. (2 Kings 4:2 NIV)

> Go, sell the oil and pay your debts. You and your sons can live off what is left. (2 Kings 4:7 NIV)

6

Vision "Go Build My Kingdom" Is Given to Me

It was the fall on 1998, and our church had scheduled a men's retreat at Pine Cove Camp just outside of Tyler, Texas. Those of us who were familiar with the area knew there were a few good golf courses around. Many of us took that Friday off and played golf near the camp prior to the opening session of the retreat. It was the first time I had been to a church camp/retreat since I was a small child. I had forgotten how much I enjoyed them.

I was well into my fourth year as a real estate professional and honestly had no business leaving my professional duties. It was a good time to get close to the Lord and deepen my relationship with Him. The first evening session ended after dinner, and we all broke to our cabins. The next morning's schedule indicated that each of us was to find a quiet place and read our Bibles, pray, and/or meditate on God's direction for our lives, our church, and the church leadership. I was being considered as a potential deacon, and I wanted to pray about how I could best serve the church.

I sprang up early the next morning, took a shower, and went to find the nearest quiet spot. I arrived at my "quiet time" spot plenty early of the scheduled start time of 7:00 a.m. I began to pray, asking the Lord where I should open His word that day. As I read my Bible, I continued to give thanks for the blessings and provision that the

Lord had given our family over the last four years. I began to pray, asking God for His direction in my life and help me further understand my purpose and the potential role of serving as a deacon at our church.

What happened next was the one and only time in my life that something like this had occurred. As I was deep in prayer, something came over my spirit, and I definitely heard the Holy Spirit say to me, "Go build my kingdom!" As I opened my eyes, I looked around to see if anyone was around or within hearing range. Nothing. I was all alone—just me and the Holy Spirit. I had goose bumps all over and was taken aback by the clarity of what had just happened. I began to flip through my Bible, looking and researching for a meaning to the directive I had just been given. I immediately found the great commission in Matthew 28:19, where Jesus states, "Therefore go and make disciples of all nations, baptizing them in the name of the Father, of the Son and of the Holy Spirit." Was that it? Was that what I was meant to do? First and foremost, yes, that applies to all of us who are believers. God has equipped each of us with special gifts and talents so that we may witness to the lost souls and bring them into His kingdom. Since that already applies to all of us, then why did the Holy Spirit say that to me? He's talking to a home builder. If he means that in a literal sense, I can build things. That's easy for me to do. Needless to say, my head was spinning trying to figure out what that meant. I left that quiet time with many questions that I had to find answers to, mainly questions like the following:

1. Why me?
2. What does "build My kingdom" mean to me?
3. What to build? How do I get them built? Where do I build them?
4. How would such a thing be paid for?
5. Or, do I build houses as my witness to spread the Gospel?

So I immediately approached my pastor, explaining what had happened during the morning quiet time. He quickly referred me to a group of local pastors who were discussing the possibility of forming a Habitat for Humanity chapter in Collin county. Having worked with Habitat for Humanity in other cities since 1987, I got involved from the start and was given an opportunity to be a founding board member and vice president of the South Collin County chapter for Habitat for Humanity in early 1998. Their motto is "Building on faith." Which means moving forward with the construction and completion of each home without knowing where the funds, the lot, the building supplies, the building materials, the volunteers, and the families will come from. It is a daily "God will provide" approach to building houses. I was quite familiar with that approach having spent the last four years living the "God will provide" approach to selling houses.

Looking back

I can clearly see the seasons of preparation in my life. First, the hands-on home building experience working in my family's business and then being in management with several national homebuilders.

Next, the big step of living on faith every single day as I prayed for my phone to ring. After the Holy Spirit spoke to me, I would spend the next twenty-two years praying and seeking the Lord's will on what he meant by "Go build My kingdom." I had to go through a season of fire and testing before I was considered ready to receive His plan. The coming eleven years of adversity and trials were the toughest I would ever experience. There were many moments where my spirit was broken, and I allowed the Lord to take over. They were turning points in my life.

After a period of refinement that spanned over fifty years, I was then ready to receive and was led to write out the concepts of His plan for me. Then when He felt the time was right, He began to reveal His plan. It came in great detail. It came in layers over a period of about six months. When the spirit led me, I would sit down and write. I would stop and then start again as each concept was revealed to me.

Each of us takes our own path through life. Some take an easy path, while I chose to take the obstacle course through life. Regardless of which path is taken, what matters most was allowing the Lord to do His work in me so that I would be equipped to carry out His will in order to further His kingdom.

The following verses encouraged me about receiving from the Holy Spirit:

> The hand of the Lord was upon me there, and He said to me, 'Get up and go out to the plain, and there I will speak to you.' (Ezekiel 3:22 NIV)

> I am the good shepherd, I know my sheep and my sheep know me. My sheep listen to my voice; I know them, and they follow me. (John 10:14, 27 NIV)

He who belongs to God hears what God says. (John 8:47 NIV)

A man can receive only what is given him from heaven. (John 3:27 NIV)

7

Provision and Confirmation—Firsthand Experience of Building on Faith with Habitat for Humanity

It was a Friday morning in October of 1999, and we were twenty-four hours away from starting the construction of our first home for the South Collin County chapter of Habitat for Humanity. Each one of the board members had a specific duty to carry out. My duty was to buy the lots and build the houses. We had just closed on our first lot, and the slab foundation was completed. The board had spent the last several weeks advertising and getting the word out that we needed volunteers to help build our first house. The goal was to have everyone show up at 8:00 a.m. on Saturday morning, and the fun would begin. We already had a temporary power pole with electricity on the lot. I had placed a shipping container on the empty lot next door to put all of the supplies and loose materials in. I had scheduled the framing package to be delivered on the first run early Saturday morning. The core group of volunteers were confirmed and committed to show up at 8:00 a.m. Everything was set and ready to go. Or so I thought. After asking around, I realized that I had forgotten to secure the supplies necessary in order to equip everyone to build the house. Supplies such as electrical cords, saws, hammers, nails, ladders, string lines, nail pouches, tape measures, framing squares, etc. How could I have missed these items?

I immediately drove to the nearest Home Depot and asked the manager if they had any supplies they could donate for our first build. Nothing. I went to Lowe's and asked their manager. Nothing. I went to Plano Lumber Yard and asked their manager. Nothing. I went to Payless Cashways and asked their manager. He took me to their back storage area and showed me a few shelves of items that had been returned that he could not resell. He told me he couldn't give them away but he would certainly sell them to us at a deep discount. That was at least a start, but still I had nothing.

By that time, it was around the noon hour, and I drove through McDonalds and bought myself a large sweet tea. I had struck out everywhere I went, and I was getting nervous. So I pulled over in the parking lot, and I began to pray that the Lord would somehow find a way and provide the supplies needed to build our first home. I continued to rack my brain and look for other stores that might be willing to donate the supplies we needed. About thirty minutes after I had prayed for the Lord's provision, my phone rang. It was Sharon, a friend of mine in the mortgage business, asking me if I was still involved with Habitat for Humanity. I said, "Yes, I am, why do you ask?" She heard that we were starting our first home the next day and wanted to participate in some way. I told her she could participate in any of the three ways that were possible. She could come out and help us build the house, she could donate supplies and other materials needed, or she could write a check as a way to help get the house built. She said that she wasn't very handy with a hammer and thought that she would just get in everybody's way. She then expressed that she would love to donate the supplies and materials needed, except she had no idea what to buy, how many, and she had no way to get them to the job site. She then asked if it was okay if she just wrote a check to Habitat and contribute that way. I said that would be absolutely okay and an answer to prayer! She said to come over to her house and there would be a check in an envelope in her mailbox with my name on it.

I couldn't get to her house fast enough. When I opened that envelope and saw a $3,000 check made payable to South Collin County Habitat for Humanity, I began to weep. I was ecstatic. I was flabbergasted. I was amazed. I was in awe. I had just witnessed the power of the Lord and His answer to my prayer for provision. As I drove back to Payless Cashways, I had goose bumps. I wept the entire way over to that store. I quickly found the manager and told him that I had money and was ready to buy all that $3,000 would get me. We loaded up shopping cart after shopping cart, and I filled up the back of my Ford Expedition three times with supplies. I made three trips to the job site, placing all the supplies inside the container for the big day ahead. I had enough electrical cords, hammers, saws, nails, ladders, string lines, nail pouches, tape measures, and framing squares for an army. We had more than we needed to get the first house completed. I had just experienced firsthand the meaning of "Building on faith."

The next morning arrived, and I opened the container, and the president of the board saw all of the supplies in the container and asked me, "Where did all of that come from?" I told him what had happened, and he had the biggest smile on his face. He was a pastor at a local church and replied, "Praise the Lord!"

We finished the first house a few weeks later, and at the hand-ing-over-the-keys ceremony on the front porch, I told everyone present the story about what building on faith meant and how it played a major role in the completion of our first home.

Our chapter has now built over one hundred homes and completed over two hundred more renovation projects around the community. God's provision has continued to bless the work of those building the houses for the families in need.

Looking back

I was just taught through firsthand experience the fundamental kingdom principle of acting out our faith. The Habitat for Humanity motto is "Building on faith." That means the leadership of each chapter is to begin building the first house, then the second house, then the third, and so on. We were taught that once we secured a lot to build on, we should begin building. We were not to worry about the funds to build each home, the supplies and materials needed to build each home, the volunteers needed to build each home, nor were we to worry about the families for each home. As long as we went out each day with the intent to build another house, God would meet our needs.

This concept that Habitat employs is counterintuitive. In the secular world, builders don't start building one house after another, then another. They prefer to mitigate their risk by waiting until they have a signed contract with a new home buyer before they spend the money for materials and subcontractors. Only then will most builders start building each house. Some of the larger homebuilders that have a good track record with their banks will build a few "spec" homes. "Spec" is short for "speculative." They sometimes will go ahead and start building a house speculating that they will sell it reasonably soon. I've seen many builders go under and file bankruptcy because they had too many "spec" homes sitting that weren't sold. What a concept! That's a normal work day for Habitat for Humanity. They spell risk f-a-i-t-h. Is it no surprise that Habitat for Humanity is the largest home builder in the world?

Habitat for Humanity employs another kingdom principle relating to the qualified families that are selected. Habitat will look for affordable lots in any given area and then build each house at their cost. They obviously have to pay for all of the materials and the mechanical subcontractors that build each home unless they are donated. Then they maximize volunteer labor to complete each house at the lowest cost possible. Finally, Habitat will provide to the new homeowner a zero-interest rate mortgage for their home with no profit built in. Compared to retail homebuilders today that charge 20 to 25 percent profit on each home along with mortgage interest, the single largest expense every homeowner with a loan encounters.

My years working with Habitat were crucial for me to really understand what it meant to build using our faith and incorporate such a foreign concept of a zero-interest mortgage! I was given a front-row seat so that I knew how to implement both concepts into the "building His kingdom" plan.

The following verses encouraged me about God's provision and confirmation:

> For the eyes of the Lord are on the righteous and His ears are attentive to their prayer. (1 Peter 3:12 NIV)

> Unless the Lord builds the house, its builders labor in vain. (Psalm 127:1 NIV)

> For it is God who works in you to will and to act according to His good purpose. (Philippians 2:13 NIV)

> And we know that in all things God works for the good of those who love Him, who have been called according to His purpose. (Romans 8:28 NIV)

8

Guidance upon Request as I Searched for My Ancestor's Grave

It was late summer of 2006, and my wife, Juli, son Wesley, and I were in Austin for a club soccer tournament. After he finished his last game on Saturday afternoon, I asked him if he wanted to go down to the UT Co-op store across the street from the university to purchase a few things. He loved that idea. After buying a few national championship items from the previous season, we had a little time to kill before heading back to the hotel. I mentioned to him that we had an ancestor who was buried in the Oakwood Cemetery across the street from the UT baseball stadium. I suggested that we take a spin through the cemetery to see if we could find his grave. He agreed, so we headed that way. Here's an aerial view of Oakwood Cemetery in Austin:

As I turned off of MLK Boulevard, I headed south on Comal Street to the entrance of the cemetery. I was not expecting the cemetery to be as large as it was. Just to provide a comparison in size, six UT baseball stadiums could fit inside Oakwood Cemetery. There were over twenty-two thousand graves in this cemetery, and I had twenty minutes left before they closed the front gates. I quickly said a little prayer, asking the Lord to help me find my great-great-great grandfather's grave. I know it was a shot in the dark, but it was worth a try. I knew this was my only chance because I had no idea when I could get back here to find it. I began to notice that there were older tombstones on one side of Comal Street and not the other, so I turned into the older section. It seemed that about every fifty feet, there were these narrow lanes that went up into the cemetery where a car could be driven through. Back then, they drove their wagons up these narrow lanes. I randomly chose one of the lanes to drive down and told my son to look at the names and look for an *X* in the name. That was an odd letter to be in someone's name, and it might help him find the tombstone a little easier. The older tombstones were covered in black fungus, and they were very hard to read. So when we came to the first set of tombstones, I rolled our windows down and told him to look out his side of the truck and I would look out of my side of the truck. As I rolled my window down, I noticed that the very first tombstone I saw had an *X* in the name. I could barely make out the name—Hedgcoxe!

Wait a minute! I put the truck in park, got out of the truck, and walked up to the tombstone and looked on the other side, and this is what I saw:

That was it. We had driven directly to my great-great-great grandfather's grave. My son Wesley noted that he had goose bumps all over and couldn't believe what he was seeing. He asked me, "Dad, how did you know his gravestone was there?" I began to weep as I knew full well how such a thing like this could happen. The Holy Spirit heard my prayer asking for direction, and He sent an angel to guide me directly to it. There's no other explanation possible. We just witnessed the power of an answer to prayer. Since we still had about fifteen minutes left before they closed the cemetery, that gave us time to take a few photos to send to the family. I was later told by other family members that no one has been able to find his grave until now.

After a few years had passed, I met a friend of mine that is a retired pastor in Fort Worth for coffee. I had the chance to tell him this story of how I found my ancestor's grave. He had one question: "Who told you to look for the *X*?" No response was needed. It wasn't luck nor coincidence. It was absolutely, without a doubt, an angel of the Lord that guided me directly to his grave.

It's been fifteen years since we found my great-great-great grandfather's grave, and I have taken other family members to see his final resting place. Each time I go there, I have trouble finding his grave. Knowing full well where it is, I have never driven straight to it like we did that day.

Looking back

Now this situation may sound a little trivial and coincidental to many. Being in my car that late afternoon was a moment I'll never forget for the rest of my life. To see the look on my son's face was beyond priceless.

I've made a point to tell all three of my boys that anything is possible in life, especially if you seek the Lord's help. My son Wesley was a little too young at the time to grasp what had just happened. He's asked me many times since then how I knew where my ancestor was buried. My response has been the same each time. I continue to tell him that I didn't know but the Lord sent an angel to guide me to the exact spot.

The Lord has a different way of preparing each of us for what He has called us to do. This was a "faith experience" that involved someone else, my son Wesley. That afternoon taught me that if I inquire to Him for something as trivial as finding a grave site, He will guide me through life. The most beautiful part is my son learned the same thing too. I was allowed to be a witness to the power of the Holy Spirit! My son can take that "faith experience" with him and build upon it as he grows closer to the Lord.

These "faith experiences" have changed me. I've learned to be more in tune with my spirit and pay more attention to my surroundings, what people are doing, and especially what people are saying. I've learned that He uses others to speak to us. At this point, I've started to develop a sense of comfort that I'm not alone. I have a greater sense of hope now than I did before.

The following verses encouraged me about seeking His guidance:

> In all your ways acknowledge Him and He will make your paths straight. (Proverbs 3:6 NIV)

> For we also had the gospel preached to us, just as they did; but the message they heard was of no value to them, because those who heard did not combine it with faith. (Hebrews 4:2 NIV)

> If any of you lacks wisdom, you should ask God, who gives generously to all without finding fault, and it will be given to you. But when you ask, you must believe and not doubt. (James 1:5–6 NIV)

9

Protected Again from Serious Injury while Driving at Night

It was a Friday night in November, and my son Wesley and I were headed to Ozona, Texas, to deer hunt. We had been given an opportunity to hunt on a large ranch and were excited to get there. Wesley played soccer, so that meant we couldn't start our seven-hour trip until after he got home from his soccer game. On this particular night, there were no clouds in the sky, and the full moon was high and bright. After about six hours on the road, we were far enough west where the speed limits were eighty miles per hour. I set my cruise control on eighty-five miles per hour and couldn't wait to get to our final destination. This time of year also means that deer like to wander out into the right of way and forage on the green grass in that area between the side of the road and the landowners' fences. As an experienced night driver, I knew that deer typically won't run across the road unless they are standing on the shoulder or very close to it. As long as they stayed well off the road, it really wasn't a big concern. This particular evening, we were seeing a large number of deer on the side of the highway. Wesley had been counting the number of deer he was seeing on his side of the highway. His deer count began to get pretty high.

What happened next most probably saved our lives. All of a sudden, this feeling came over me to slow down and pay very close attention to the deer on the road. So I slowed down to forty-five miles per hour and told Wesley to start paying very close attention to his side of the highway and watch even closer for deer. I began to do the same on my side of the road. We came around a corner and began a long straight stretch of highway. This particular highway was one lane on both sides with only a center stripe. As we started down the long stretch, I could see the headlights of an approaching car down in the distance. I continued to watch closely for deer on my side of the road. As the approaching car got closer and closer, it created a blind spot directly in front of me where I couldn't see if there were any deer until after the car passed by.

Finally, the car passed by, and a large buck deer was standing broadside in the middle of the highway, facing the opposite direction. After the car passed me, the deer took two steps out into the middle of my lane just before I hit him. It happened so fast I was not able to hit my brakes and hit the deer at full speed. Fortunately for us, it was only forty-five miles per hour. After putting the car in park, Wesley and I got out of the car in the middle of the lonely highway to see the damage. It was horrible. The front end of my car was destroyed, and, needless to say, the deer didn't survive either. As best as I could tell, my car would still run, but I didn't know for how long. It was a miracle the deer didn't go through my windshield. If I had been going eighty-five miles per hour, it most certainly would have and most likely injured both of us significantly. I had only reduced my speed forty-five miles per hour just less than a half a mile prior to hitting that deer. Wesley asked me, "Dad, how did you know to slow down?" We both had goose bumps, and I began to weep because I knew that the Lord's angel was protecting us that night and caused me to slow down. There was no other explanation that made any sense. We were both very lucky to have survived that incident, and I thanked the Lord for His presence that night on that lonely highway.

Looking back

Similar to the incident when I was digging the postholes for my fence, there was a clear intervention that caused me to act unnaturally. For no apparent reason, I slowed down to forty-five miles per hour that night. Something came over me that I cannot explain.

That was now the second time in two years Wes was with me as we witnessed the power of the Holy Spirit and His angels. He later commented that riding in the car with Dad is never boring!

When we arrived at deer camp, everyone was eager to hear what happened to my car. As I told them the chronology of events, there was an overwhelming response from the group that God was watching out over the two of us that night. Each of them had stories to tell where their own encounters with deer along a night highway ended very differently.

By now it has become clear that the Lord has plans for me and my son Wesley. We now get up every morning thanking Him for the hope that He has given us and the encouragement that His word brings.

The following verses encouraged me about the Lord's angels protecting me:

> For He will command His angels concerning you to guard you in all your ways; they will lift you up in their hands, so that you will not strike your foot against a stone." (Psalm 91:11–12 NIV)

> Give thanks in all circumstances; for this is God's will for you in Christ Jesus. (1 Thessalonians 5:18 NIV)

> Praise Him, all His angels; praise Him, all His heavenly hosts. (Psalms 148:2 NIV)

10

Provision, Guidance, and Blessing during Weekly Prayer Calls

Being in the real estate business, I meet some interesting people. I often get introduced to business opportunities that are outside of real estate. I've been approached to participate in countless deals and have learned to "stay in my lane" and stick with real estate. Over the years, I have "connected" with a few gentlemen in various parts of the country that are like-minded Christians with a good heart striving to live godly lives. We would sometimes get on the phone together to pray and encourage one another with current activities and opportunities, pray for the Lord's guidance, provision, and blessings. We began to appreciate each of the calls and decided that we would have a scheduled conference call together once a week at the same time. There were typically six of us on each call, three of whom were ordained ministers. Each of us would tell what was going on in our lives and ask for others to pray for them. Many times we would receive words of encouragement and much-needed wisdom from the group.

After getting comfortable with everyone on the call, I told them the story of how the Holy Spirit had spoken to my spirit and walked away from a men's retreat with a directive to "go build My kingdom." I asked them to pray and help me understand what that meant. I had many questions and needed clarity on this topic. They all agreed that they would seek the Lord's will on the subject and pray that He would enlighten me with answers.

Now from time to time, if one encountered an individual that others felt worthy of joining us on the call, that person was invited to join in. We would listen and encourage that person and ask how we could bless them and their family.

On one particular scheduled call, there were four other persons that were invited to be on our weekly call. I did not know any of them as they were invited by another one of our regulars. The topic of the conversation that particular day was about various different ways to fund a project. Such as a large multitiered real estate transaction, a mining opportunity, or an oil/gas transaction. This was a topic I knew nothing about, so I just listened the entire time. On the call was a woman named Cindy, and she had experience with financial instruments like bonds, notes, etc. She began to speak of an upcoming global event and mentioned that all of us should start paying attention to this. For some reason, that grabbed my attention, and I began to listen intently as she spoke about details she had received from her attorney who was directly involved in the event.

After the call, I immediately reached out to one of the other weekly regulars that lived in Houston, and we both agreed that it might be in our best interest to meet with this woman named Cindy and learn more about the upcoming global event. So we met at a location in Dallas the very next day. My friend Kent drove up from Houston, and Cindy drove in from a small town south of Dallas. Cindy began to provide many details of the coming global event and explained to us just what that meant, why it had to occur, and, with it, a little history lesson to back it up. Apparently, her attorney had been doing other business with a previous government leader that happened to live in Dallas. Her back door channels of information seemed to provide information and opportunities that the general public didn't know existed. One of those opportunities was a chance to participate directly in the event. After doing much due diligence on the subject, my friend and I agreed to participate in the event ourselves. We immediately had to sign a nondisclosure agreement with those involved and are strictly forbidden to discuss anything about it to others. Hopefully, at a later time, I will be able to speak of the details of this event. I want others to see the Lord's hand at work.

Looking back

One morning, I received a phone call from Al, a gentleman whom I've not talked to in over ten years. He asked if he could come to my office as he had something he wanted to talk to me about. Upon arrival, he disclosed to me that he is an intercessor. During his daily prayer time, he said that the Holy Spirit revealed to him that I would receive a great blessing larger than I could comprehend. After a brief discussion and prayer together, he left. About a month later, he asked if he could return to my office. After indicating that he had been praying for me and my business, he reemphasized that the Holy Spirit revealed to him a second time that I would receive a large blessing in my life. He didn't mention any specifics about what kind of blessing it could be.

Being able to witness His amazing ability to weave His will through others' lives and fit it all together according to His glorious plan is incredible. I never cease to be amazed at how awesome our Lord is. There's not a day that goes by that I don't praise Him and lift Him up!

The following verses encouraged me about His provision, guidance, and blessings:

> Again, truly I tell you that if two of you on earth agree about anything they ask for, it will be done for them by my Father in heaven. For where two or three gather in my name, there I am with them. (Matthew 18:19–20 NIV)

> Plans fail for lack of counsel, but with many advisors they succeed. (Proverbs 15:22 NIV)

> Let us go with you, because we have heard that God is with you. (Zechariah 8:23 NIV)

> For the eyes of the Lord are on the righteous and His ears are attentive to their prayer. (1 Peter 3:12 NIV)

11

Guidance, Protection, and Gratitude as I'm Directed to *the* Emergency Room

It was early February of 2017, and I was about to complete an eighteen-month stint as an energy consultant with a local energy-rating firm. During the term, my job required that I drive approximately one hour to the main offices in Irving from 6:30 a.m. to noon every day. Then I could carry on with my real estate duties after noon. This particular Monday morning would be different.

After getting out of the shower, I walked into my bedroom to put my clothes on. After grabbing my socks, I accidentally dropped them on the floor. I reached down to pick them up. As I was coming up, something happened. I lost my breath and struggled to breathe for a good ten minutes. I began to sweat profusely as I tried to catch my breath. I sat down on the edge of the bed and slowly tried to gain my composure and breathe normally. Finally, I gained control of myself, but something wasn't right. I was only able to breathe shallow breaths, and my chest began to tighten. It didn't get any worse, but it didn't improve either. After about fifteen more minutes, I walked to my car and began the hour drive to the office in Irving. I realize now that was not a smart decision! Upon arrival, I grabbed my backpack and made my way up the flight of stairs to my office. Walking up one flight of stairs seemed impossible, but after a couple of minutes, I made it to my office. After only a few minutes, my officemate looked at me and said, "You don't look very good."

I replied, "I don't feel very good either." Well, the power of positive thinking didn't make my shallow breathing go away, so I decided that I should leave and find an emergency room. The question was which emergency room. I said a prayer, asking the Lord to direct me to the right hospital. I just began to drive back to the Plano area, about thirty minutes away. Then I suddenly realized there was a heart hospital in south Plano near Preston Road and the Bush turnpike. I deducted that was a good place to go since my symptoms were presenting themselves as heart related. Rather than drive up to the door at the emergency room, I decided to just park out in their parking lot and walk in. Again, another unsmart decision. It took forever for me to walk the fifty yards to the door of the hospital. Just prior to walking in the emergency room, I called my wife, Juli, and told her she may want to come over to the hospital.

After answering a few detailed questions, the medical staff immediately whisked me into a trauma room and began asking me questions and poking holes in me. After their two-minute drill on me, they began to assume I had a mild heart attack. After further testing, they admitted me to the "Heart Hospital" of Plano. Unbeknownst to me, I had driven to the only hospital in north Texas that was 100 percent attended by cardiologists. Every doctor in this hospital was an expert on all matters of the heart. Did I come to the right place? I didn't know what was wrong with me, but I felt assured that I had landed in the best place possible. They conducted an angioplasty procedure on me and found no blockage and no damage to my heart. The cardiologist that performed the procedure said that I had the heart of a fifteen-year-old. That was great news! But they still didn't know what the problem was. Then they performed a CT scan on me. They put iodine in my veins and put me through an MRI machine, and that's when they found them!

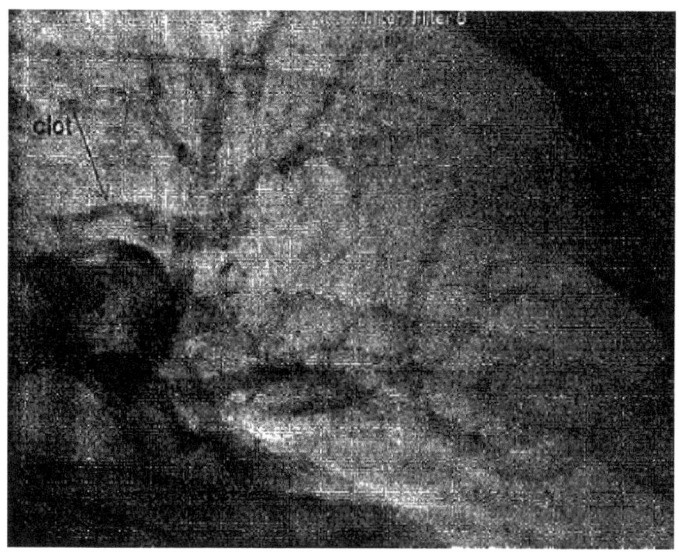

Blood clots! Three of them. One in each lung, and one in my heart. After I woke up in my room, the doctor came in and began to draw a very detailed cross section of the human heart on the whiteboard in my room. He drew a little circle on the top valve of my heart and said, "That's where the blood clot is in your heart." He added that I had an additional blood clot in each lung. The very next words out of his mouth were "You are very lucky to be alive right now. Fifty percent of the patients with this condition never make it to the emergency room. You have a pulmonary embolism, or emboli since there are several of them." After returning to my room about an hour later, the cardiologist informed me that he wanted to do a procedure that required placing small hollow wires into the carotid arteries in my neck and dispense a clot-busting medicine known as TPA into each lung, directly on top of each clot. He added that after approximately sixteen hours, the medicine would dissolve the clots. They were able to dissolve the clot in my heart by administering blood thinners intravenously while the TPA was doing its job in my lungs. The small round ends of the wires can be seen below where the TPA clot-busting medicine is dispensed:

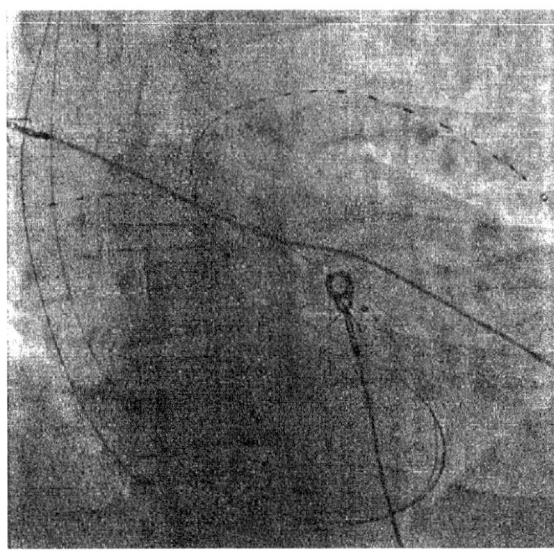

After approximately twenty hours, they came into my room and began removing the wires in my neck. Another cardiologist came into my room to give me the good news. The clots were gone! Praise the Lord! He immediately asked me, "How did you know to come to this hospital?"

I responded by saying, "I have no idea, why?"

The doctor responded by saying, "We are one of only two hospitals in the DFW metroplex that will do the TPA procedure on patients. You are most fortunate to have come here without knowing that. Do you realize how lucky you are?"

The cardiologist that performed the procedure on me came into my room a little while later. He was very happy with the results. He added that he had performed that procedure eight times within the last year and the results were positive six of the eight times. I asked about the other two times, and he said that the patients didn't survive. He added, "The Lord must have special plans for you because you are very lucky to be alive." I remained in intensive care for an additional forty-eight hours for observation. Every shift, the cardiologists made their rounds and stepped into my room. Each one of them would read my chart and say, "Wow, do you know how lucky you are?" After five to six comments along those lines, I began to realize just how fortunate I was. It wasn't luck—the Lord heard my prayer that morning asking for direction to the right hospital, and the Lord sent an angel to direct my path to the best heart doctors in the DFW area that saved my life!

After conducting a little research on hospitals in the northeastern portion of the DFW metroplex, I concluded that I had a 1 percent chance of walking out of that hospital alive given all of the circumstances. Now it was up to me to make the doctors' efforts worth it. I was most thankful with a new vigor for life and was determined to make the most of it!

Looking back

By now each "faith experience" seemed to reinforce the others to the point where even an atheist would believe. This "event," as the medical profession likes to call it, was a real turning point in my life. I walked out of that hospital a different person. I was shaken to the core at the events that took place and how I was led to *the* hospital.

I eagerly began to seek the Lord each day, giving thanks for saving me and inquiring of Him to show me His plan for me. Over the next three years, He would do exactly that!

He laid it on my fifteen-year-old heart that I was to start walking. My fifty-seven-year-old body, bad habits and all, needed to heal. I started out with the ability to walk one-fourth of a mile at a time. I patiently increased the distance as my body would allow it. I began to really enjoy walking outside in the sunshine. I found that long walks healed my mind and healed my body. I learned that for those of us over fifty years of age, walking every other day speeds up weight loss as compared to walking every day. My body needed the extra day to rest and heal before walking again. I'm happy to say that I was able to work my distance up to just over four miles. It's an hour that I most enjoy and look forward to three days a week!

The following verses encouraged me about His guidance and protection and about my gratitude:

> For He will command His angels concerning you to guard you in all your ways; they will lift you up in their hands, so that you will not strike your foot against a stone. (Psalm 91:11–12 NIV)

> 'For I know the plans I have for you,' declares the Lord, 'plans to prosper you and not to harm you, plans to give you hope and a future.' (Jeremiah 29:11 NIV)

> But be sure to fear the Lord and serve him faithfully with all your heart; consider what great things he has done for you. (1 Samuel 12:24 NIV)

> Praise Him, all His angels; praise Him, all His heavenly hosts. (Psalms 148:2 NIV)

12

Affirmation and Blessings after Taking God Up on His Promise

After coming home from the hospital and miraculously being cured of multiple blood clots, in many ways, I had hit bottom. I was morbidly obese and could hardly walk around the nurses' station before leaving the hospital. I was given several prescriptions that supposedly helped my condition but slowed my metabolism and increased my weight gain. My income had dramatically fallen off due to the fact that I had stopped prospecting for real estate business back in 2008. We were basically broke—with no money in the bank and nothing saved in case of a rainy day. My energy rater term was about to expire, and that meant I had to go hunting for food again. I was paid a small salary for being an energy rater. When selling real estate, it's like being unemployed every day. Money doesn't come in unless I go out and sell something. Up until that point, I believed that my income was performance based. For the last twenty-three years, 100 percent of my income was commissions. That created a lot of fear and stress that added to my weight gain over the years. I was at a crossroads in my life, and I needed something to change quickly. It was time to take my own advice that I've told my three sons. I've always told them, "If you keep doing the same thing, you'll keep getting the same results. If you want different results, you'll need to make significant changes in your life." It was definitely time for me to make a structural change to my life, and I was willing to do just that.

After having just experienced a miracle with my health, we needed more where those came from. The Lord had my attention, and I was willing to do whatever it took to turn things around. If that meant doing something I've never done, then I was willing to do it. Interestingly enough, our pastor had just discussed the concept and meaning behind tithing, and it really convicted me on just where our source of income is derived. I would consider tithing, except I had very little income. We needed every single cent to live off of, and even that wasn't enough. I knew that tithing was the ultimate act of worship and trust in the Lord, and for the first time in my life, I was willing to take the Lord up on His promise.

So after receiving my last few paychecks as an energy rater, I began to tithe. The weekly checks made the tithes smaller, and that made the transition a little easier for what was about to come. I knew that the next few weeks were about to be slim pickings since I had not done any prospecting for a buyer or seller in almost ten years. I truly needed another one of those miracles.

After my energy rater term ended, I was back to being unemployed every day with a real estate license in my back pocket. I began to reintroduce myself to some of my past clients. The phone began to ring ever so slowly, and I began to see some activity with my business. It was a true miracle that my phone rang at all. I began to close homes and then the hard part started. Upon receiving my commission check, I would then need to make a one-time tithe to my church based upon the entire net commissions earned. That was a lot more than a weekly salary paycheck! This is where the rubber met the road with me, and I nervously began making those much larger tithes upon receiving my commission checks. As each month went by, my wife and I started to notice that we weren't having to scrimp for every dollar to go buy food, gas, or pay the rent. It wasn't a lot, but we started to see a little relief from before. It was at that point that my wife, Juli, began to tithe her paychecks every two weeks.

As the commission checks kept coming in, I would immediately make the tithe each time. I started to notice something very unusual. In some cases, the same day or the next day after making the tithe, my phone would ring, and it would be a buyer wanting to buy a home or a seller wanting to list their home. These people that were calling me had not heard from me in almost ten years! I wasn't doing anything to cause them to call me. They were just calling me out of the blue, asking if I was still selling real estate and saying they needed to use my services. I would be sitting at a red light (or a green light as Zig Ziglar used to say) and yell, "Wow, thank you, Lord!" Those calls were coming out of nowhere. I had done nothing to deserve those commission checks. I track the sources of all of my real estate transactions, and there began a string of sales that were from past clients from long ago that just called me with no rhyme nor reason for why they called me. I can truly say each one of them was a blessing from the Lord!

After seeing this pattern of blessings after tithing each time, that strengthened my faith. The more money I made, the more I was willing to tithe. I was starting to become that cheerful giver I had read about since childhood.

Looking back

It's taken me over fifty-five years to shake the preconceived ideas that I had about tithing. I had to come to the realization that the Lord doesn't need my money. He's after my heart. It's an act of obedience that opens the doors to heaven.

It's been a few years since we began tithing, and He has blessed Juli and I immensely. I think it's fair to say that I tested the Lord, and He has kept His word with me. He has continued to bless us financially as well as in other ways. We both have a peace about our financial situation that we've never had before. I don't get anxious about financial matters because I know that the Lord is in control.

Once we began tithing,

- my relationship with Jesus grew stronger,
- the Lord began to heal my body,
- my real estate business improved without me doing a thing,
- Juli's income increased because more Realtors wanted to use her services and appreciated her servant heart,
- our love for one another is stronger now than it ever has been,
- the Lord revealed to me what "Go build My kingdom" meant,
- my friend Cindy asked me to put together my thoughts to give to her grandson John Bates,
- the Lord's angels repeatedly confirmed their presence in my life,
- an intercessor came to me twice to tell me about what the Lord had revealed to him about a future blessing I was to receive,
- my life came back together better than it was before,
- all of our needs were exceedingly met, and
- we have been extremely blessed, and I can narrow it down to the very day we first began to tithe our incomes.

I regret living all these years in disobedience without understanding where our source of income is derived. I have missed out on so many years of a deepened faith and His blessings. They are years that I can't get back, and I want my sons to know that the scriptures are true. He has made believers out of us.

The following verses gave me great encouragement and affirmation regarding blessings from the Lord:

> The earth is the Lord's and everything in it, the world and all who live in it for He founded it upon the seas and established it upon the waters. (Psalm 24:1–2 NIV)

> "Test me in this," says the Lord Almighty, "and see if I will not throw open the floodgates of heaven and pour out so much blessing that there will not be room enough to store it." (Malachi 3:10 NIV)

> But remember the Lord your God, for it is He who gives you the ability to produce wealth. (Deuteronomy 8:18 NIV)

> And my God will meet all of your needs according to His glorious riches in Christ Jesus. (Philippians 4:19 NIV)

13

Healing during a Time of Recovery

Immediately after my pulmonary embolism episode, I had to take things very slowly for quite a while. My cardiologist had administered several prescription medications that were attempting to get me on the right track to full recovery. My weight had crept up, and it didn't seem to be going down. I had a hard time getting up from a seated position without struggling a bit. I slowly began to start walking on a periodic basis to improve my mobility. I started with a very simple one-fourth-mile walk. After several weeks, I increased it up to one-half mile. After one month, I increased that up to one mile. Then up to one and a half miles, and six weeks later, I bumped it up to two and a half miles. At my one-year checkup with my cardiologist, I was able to get around a three-mile circuit in my neighborhood three times per week. I told my doctor how I was progressing with my walking but my weight wasn't going down. He reevaluated my prescription medications and determined that two of the medications were slowing down my metabolism. He decided to remove those so I could hopefully make significant progress in losing some weight. He thought it would be a great idea if I could lose twenty pounds or so and consider intermittent fasting as a method to accomplish that goal. I told him I wanted to lose fifty pounds by the next yearly checkup. He high-fived me and sent me on my way.

The very next month after my annual doctor's visit, I attended my fortieth high school reunion. At the end of the evening, those of us that were in attendance that played ball in college got together for a quick photo. My classmates began circulating this photo afterward so that each of us had a copy. My first look at this photo made me want to run and hide. I asked, "Who is that grossly overweight guy in the middle of the photo?" I knew the answer—it was most definitely me. I had never experienced shame and humiliation like this before. I was absolutely horrified. Did I really look like that? I went home and found the scales and jumped on them. I weighed 335 pounds! Oh my goodness! I wanted to crawl into a hole and not come out. I wanted to stop eating at that moment.

Now I had tried and lost a little bit of weight in the past and was somewhat successful. Quite honestly, it didn't produce long-term results. I still didn't know how to properly eat while losing weight. I began to ask the Lord for His direction on the best way for me to lose weight. I began to research the various different programs out there and their approach to losing weight and keeping it off. My fifty-ninth birthday was approaching later the next month. I had already determined that I was going to start my new weight loss program the day after Thanksgiving since my birthday was the day before Thanksgiving. There's no better way to kick-start a new lifestyle than to overeat on Thanksgiving Day and have that miserable feeling of gluttony.

After much prayer and consternation, I needed a simple but effective approach that I could see myself committing to every day without fail. After several weeks of prayer and review, I had found my solution and was ready to start the day after Thanksgiving.

One of my favorite movies is *The Shawshank Redemption*. In that movie, Morgan Freemen's character has just been released from prison, and he was at a crossroads in his life. He had to decide if he was going to move forward or slip back into his old ways. He most famously said, "Get busy living or get busy dying!" I decided right then and there that I was going to get busy living.

I had put together my eating plan, my exercise plan, and my sleeping plan. I had a daily regimen of vitamins, supplements, and electrolytes to aid in my new health plan. My goal was to lose 125 pounds by my sixtieth birthday. That's exactly one year from my start date. The shame of seeing that photo kept me extremely motivated. I thought through my plan and learned from my previous attempts at losing weight. I decided that if the weight was going to stay off, I needed to learn how to manage my weight, not just lose the weight. I knew that if I deprived myself along the way, after reaching my goal, I would be inclined to go eat everything that I had missed out on. So after the first month, I lost 25 pounds, and we went out and ate a hamburger or two. After getting back on the scales Monday morning, I had gained 4 pounds. I immediately went back to my routine, and by Thursday, I had lost the 4 pounds. The next month, I lost another 15 pounds, so we went out and ate Mexican food. Monday morning's weigh-in showed that I had gained 3 pounds. I immediately went back to my routine, and by Thursday, I had lost the 3 pounds. Each time I reached a milestone, we went out and celebrated. Each Monday morning, I would notice the price I paid, and by Thursday, I was back to where I started. I continued that approach until my birthday. By the time I had reached my sixtieth birthday, I had gained 63 pounds, due to my cheat weekends, while I lost a gross total of 188 pounds. I weighed in at 210 pounds. I had reached my goal weight on the date I had set.

 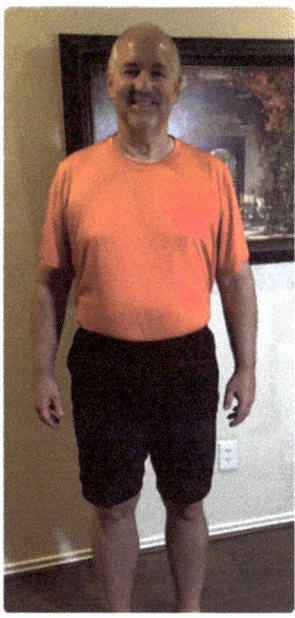

The photo above is after ten months when I had lost a net of 100 pounds. I would go on to lose an additional 25 pounds.

I paid a price for learning how to manage my weight. I lost 63 pounds twice during that time in order to accomplish my goal. Weighing every day gave me the instant feedback I needed in order to stay on track. The most important part was having the confidence that I could manage my weight on a daily or weekly basis and live along the way!

Here's how I tracked my progress:

Net Pounds Lost	Additional Pounds Gained
25 lbs	4 lbs
40 lbs	3 lbs
50 lbs	5 lbs
60 lbs	4 lbs
75 lbs	8 lbs (extended holiday vacation)
80 lbs	3 lbs
90 lbs	4 lbs
100 lbs	15 lbs (another extended holiday vacation)
110 lbs	9 lbs
115 lbs	8 lbs
125 lbs	0 lbs
	63 extra lbs

Summary	
Total Weight Lost	188 lbs
Additional Weight Gained	63 lbs
Net Weight Lost	125 lbs

Honestly, I was amazed. I had never believed that I could conquer such a task at my age. Juli and I went to dinner and then to church to celebrate Christmas and my healing.

Juli kept commenting that after knowing me for thirty-eight years, she had never seen me this focused and committed to anything. Accomplishing that amount of weight loss took significant effort on my part. Effort that I didn't know that I had. It took an extreme amount of mental strength to follow a plan as strictly as I followed mine and stick with it to the end. That's what shame will do.

Overeating was a stronghold that had its grip on me, and I was never able to shake it loose. Not until I went to the Lord for help. The answer was quite simple. I prayed that the Holy Spirit would answer my prayer of learning how to lose weight properly and be able to maintain a healthy weight afterward. I truly believe that the Lord sent His angels to place that doctor in front of me at that specific time of my life. I listened to that doctor and what he had to say about the cause and effect of what you eat, how much you eat, and when you eat it. I had never seen this doctor before, but he had my full attention just at the right moment in time. I continued to follow that doctor and his recommendations for the entire year. I learned and implemented so many aspects of his teachings into my daily life that cost me absolutely nothing. The most important thing I learned was that the body can't effectively lose weight and maintain that weight loss unless it heals first. Once I understood how to heal my body, I began to lose weight and keep it off.

It's been over one year since I reached my goal weight of 210 pounds. I'm happy to say that I'm still at my goal weight and have learned how to maintain it. When it came time for my yearly checkup with my cardiologist, I weighed in at 220 pounds. That was a few weeks prior to my deadline. Needless to say, he was amazed and couldn't believe my results. He kept saying that my results were just "outstanding," and he said it over and over again the entire time I was in his office. I counted a total of five times he described my results as "outstanding." He was ecstatic. I had tears running down my cheeks to see the man who saved my life when I had the pulmonary embolism event be so pleased with my results. That meant a lot to me!

Looking back

Gaining all of that weight was a result of me being out of control. It's amazing to me that when I looked at myself in the mirror every morning as I brushed my teeth and combed my hair, I still didn't see. My priorities were out of balance. My eating habits were horrendous. I didn't exercise at all. I continued to stress out about my real estate business. I had wandered away from the Lord. I was one cookie away from dying.

As I previously mentioned, I had tried the low-fat diets and others, but I never really understood what causes weight gain. Much to my surprise, it's not as simple as calories in and calories out. I considered those weight loss clinics, but I didn't want a quick fix. I needed a long-term solution. My problem was between my ears.

Once I said a prayer asking the Lord to reveal to me a plan that I could understand and commit to, I began to believe. I spent an entire month educating myself on the cause and effect of eating different types of foods. I had to learn some basic terms of the endocrine and digestive systems that explain what causes the body to gain weight. Terms such as intermittent fasting, insulin resistance, glycation, autophagy, and ascites. None of these terms I had heard before. Why was this not part of our junior high health class? That's when I began to realize we are brought up in a society watching television advertisements that promote unhealthy foods while preying on the uninformed. I was one of the uninformed. That was about to change.

I reached out to a couple of friends that had previous success losing significant amounts of weight on the keto plan. I learned from their experiences and from the doctor I was following and put together a solid plan of eating, exercising, vitamins/supplements, and sleeping. By the time my birthday arrived, I was more than ready to begin.

In just over a month and a half, I had the perfect plan in place to successfully reach my goal weight. I had the *motivation* to change my habits. I was *committed* to my goal of losing 125 pounds. Most importantly, with the Lord's help, I was given a *plan* that would change my life for the better.

Losing all that weight was a significant building block on my journey back. It was most certainly a turning point. I regained the confidence in myself which would translate to every aspect of my life.

The following verses encouraged me through my challenges while healing:

> Do not stay in the stronghold. Go into the land of Judah. (1 Samuel 22:5 NIV)

> We went through fire and water, but you brought us to a place of abundance. (Psalm 66:12 NIV)

I will refine them like silver and test them like gold. They will call My name and I will answer them; I will say, 'They are My people,' and they will say, 'The Lord is our God.' (Zechariah 13:9 NIV)

He rescued me because He delighted in me. (2 Samuel 22:20 NIV)

14

Rescued from Dark Times by an Angel

Just to provide a perspective on my outlook on life, I have always been the one whose glass was half full, never half empty. I approached everything as an adventure, willing to accept any and all challenges that life had to offer. I was a two-time graduate of Zig Ziglar's *See You at the Top* training series. I was professionally trained to have a positive mental attitude and very happy to use it. I loved life. People would tell me they loved being around me, and my positive attitude rubbed off on them.

Starting in October of 2008, a series of events took place in my life where I found myself in a mental state that I had never been before. It was guilt. Guilt brought on by wishing I had done more to help someone I love dearly. Unknowingly, I allowed Satan to take a foothold in my life. I began a downward spiral that I couldn't shake. I was diagnosed with severe mental depression and was given medication to numb the pain. Nothing seemed to work as there were months upon months where I laid in bed in a fetal position, trying to escape the pain. I eventually was able to get out of bed on a semi-regular basis but would sit on the couch with a blank stare at the television. I'm told I never left that couch on a daily basis for over a year. I had lost any concept of time, nor did I care.

My day job as a real estate professional came to a standstill. Potential clients would call me, but I did not have the capacity to assist them. I lost my ability to care. I didn't care about anything. At the time, I didn't care if I stopped living. Yes, there were days when I considered the unthinkable. I continued to refer potential clients to my coworkers because they were in a better position to help than I was. As my phone continued to ring, I continued to disappear. I went almost ten years without contacting my past clients. Most of them thought I either moved away or retired.

During this period, I began to make some very poor decisions. Decisions that would cost me my house, valuable relationships with friends, family members, and millions of dollars in lost real estate income. I began to gain weight due to stress eating. My health was starting to decline significantly. Even when I wanted to get off the couch, it became a challenge due to lack of mobility.

In 2013, my son Brandon had rescued a dog in college, and he needed us to take the dog for a while. My wife and I gladly accepted and flew out to California to bring the dog home. This dog was around five years old, fifty-plus pounds and a ball of energy. She was a terrier mix with quite a bit of pit bull in her. She was the sweetest living soul I had ever encountered. Her unconditional love and ability to jump up in my lap and hold me when I needed it the most was a gift from God. I affectionately named her Baby Puppy. The emotional attachment had begun.

One morning I received an email from my real estate broker. He was severing our working agreement due to the fact that I had not paid him in over a year. I had no idea that I owed him a ridiculous amount of money. He would send me my monthly statements, but I would never open them because I just didn't care enough. However, that email got my attention. I was about to be unemployed for sure if I didn't make some changes. What other broker would want to take on this sad case? I convinced my broker that I would start turning things around and he would see positive results within sixty days. I began to have one small success at a time, and every day when I came home, my four-legged ball of energy was happy to see me and sit in my lap and hold me. Those moments began to turn me around. I have never been emotionally attached to a pet in my entire life, but this one was different. She began to get under my skin. The small successes and my daily doses of Baby Puppy got me off the couch, out of the house, and being productive again. I eventually got off my medication and started to feel normal again.

Moving forward, I was able to get caught up and pay my broker the money that I owed him, lose the massive amount of weight that I had gained, and I had a much better outlook on life. I can most certainly look back and point to one moment where my life began to turn around for the better, and that is the day my Baby Puppy rescued me. I truly believe that the Lord brought her into our lives so she could rescue me from the grips of Satan. She literally saved my life.

Baby Puppy

It wasn't very long after my rescue that she developed an inoperable cancer, and we eventually had to put her down. Once I realized that I could handle her passing, I knew that the Lord has restored me after many years living in depression. I thank God every day for the angel He brought into my life!

Looking back

As I reflect back on the eleven years of my "desert experience," I realize that the Lord took me through the desert for the privilege to be used in His kingdom. He took away everything in my life and was willing to take as long as necessary to bring me back. I had to hit rock bottom. During that time, I experienced the lowest point in my life spiritually, mentally, financially, physically, and professionally. I had reached the end of the road. It's there at the end of the road where I focused on one thing—Jesus.

It amazes me that the Lord can use a dog to heal the mind. At the time, I thought we were doing my son Brandon a favor by bringing his dog back to Texas. In turns out Brandon did us the favor. I am absolutely convinced that Baby Puppy was one of God's angels sent to heal us.

The following verses encouraged me during my desert experience:

> Hand this man over to Satan for the destruction of the flesh, so that his spirit may be saved on the day of the Lord. (1 Corinthians 5:5 NIV)

> Those who sow with tears will reap with songs of joy. Those who go out weeping, carrying seed to sow, will return with songs of joy. (Psalm 126:5–6 NIV)

> The weapons we fight with are not the weapons of the world. On the contrary, they have divine power to demolish strongholds." (2 Corinthians 10:4 NIV)

If we confess our sins, he is faithful and just and will forgive us our sins and purify us from all unrighteousness. (1 John 1:9 NIV)

He brought me out into a spacious place; he rescued me because he delighted in me. (2 Samuel 22:20 NIV)

15

The Finger of God—the Lord's Testimony of Provision

Coming out of those dark times was a period of hope and rebuilding. We were living paycheck to paycheck and struggling to make ends meet. There were paychecks where we had $50 for groceries for the two of us. I remember having to borrow money just to put gas in my car. We didn't have the financial ability to do anything or go anywhere. My poor decisions from the past were causing a significant amount of suffering. Thankfully, my wife hung in there as we were going through our own "desert experience." Our faith was being tested. It took all of the patience and perseverance we could muster just to get through each day. By that time, we had leveraged car titles, payday loans, and were masters at playing the float.

There came a day when I had no real estate transactions in title with a mountain of bills that had to be paid. My car insurance had been terminated for nonpayment, and my electricity was about to be cut off for the third time. I didn't have the money to pay the rent that was due, and our phone service was about to be cut off for nonpayment—again. My truck was in disrepair and needed $2,500 just to make it go around the block. It had come to a head. I had nowhere to go, my money options had been exhausted. I got down on my knees and told God he had my full attention. I prayed for relief. I prayed that He would provide a way to help us out of this situation.

At the end of the next day, my wife walked in with the mail. She said I had received something in the mail. It was an envelope from a gentleman down in Central Texas that I had met over fifteen years ago. I opened up the envelope, and there was a check for $12,250! Apparently, after just making an introduction, I was given an equity position in a commercial office building, and that was my share of the sales proceeds. I immediately got on the phone to call and confirm what I was seeing. Hallelujah! It was confirmed. There was no other way to say it—God found a way! His timing was nothing short of a miracle. He provided a way to help us so we could move forward. That was a very significant moment in my Christian walk. To have a check of that size show up in my mailbox the very next day after giving it all to Him was an incredible moment in my life that I will never forget!

Approximately six months had gone by, and we were still trying to lift ourselves out of the pit we were in. We were in almost the identical situation as before. The funds we had were gone, no new real estate income on the horizon, and the bills were piling up. I got down on my knees and asked God's help again. This time I received a phone call. It was a past commercial real estate broker friend of mine from the DFW area. He called to advise me that the property I had referred clients to over ten years ago had just closed, and he was mailing me a check for $8,700. I had totally forgotten about the property and didn't know it was even for sale. My faith experiences continued to build. God continued to show us that if we would just be obedient and seek Him, he would bless our path.

Looking back

There's no question—God revealed His power by turning two seemingly impossible situations into glorious faith experiences.

I've come to understand the difference between a personal testimony and the Lord's testimony. A personal testimony is a faith experience where I may have done one thing or another. The Lord's testimony is when timely events occur without me being involved in any way. They supernaturally occur. That was the case here. In both instances, those checks arrived without my knowledge, direction, or involvement. Their timing was from God.

Praise the Lord!

The following verses inspired and encouraged me as I witnessed the Lord's testimony:

> When the Lord finished speaking to Moses on Mt. Sinai, He gave him the two tablets of the Testimony, the tablets of stone inscribed by the finger of God. (Exodus 31:18 NIV)

> He stilled the storm to a whisper; the waves of the sea were hushed. They were glad when it grew calm, and He guided them to their desired haven. (Psalm 107:29–30 NIV)

> If you are pleased with me, teach me your ways so I may know you and continue to find favor with you. (Exodus 33:13 NIV)

16

Revelation as "Build My Kingdom" Is Given to Me in Great Detail

It has been just over twenty-three years since I had that special moment with God in the middle of the East Texas woods. I remember that moment as clearly now as I did when it occurred. I have continued to pray and ask the Lord to provide me the details on what He meant by "Go build My kingdom." I have also asked that if I have somehow fallen out of favor and am no longer considered, please let that be known to me.

Over a period of about six months, the Lord began to convey many things to me in great detail. I opened up my laptop, and I began to write.

The concepts came to me in layers. These are concepts that I understood but I've never discussed or written about in my life. Concepts such as the following:

- How to build totally sustainable simple homes in forty-eight hours in all twelve climate zones around the world that will last one hundred plus years
- How to build net zero retail housing in less than thirty days for all first-time buyers around the world at a cost that is 30–35 percent lower than today's homes
- Manufacturing and transportation solutions for the aforementioned sustainable homes worldwide using various methods to build, deliver, and complete on-site
- Build community multipurpose facilities and churches providing for education, health care, exercise, local jobs and job training, hydroponics/vertical farming
- How to renovate older substandard housing and provide safe drinking water, sanitary sewer, and electricity currently occupied by the elderly around the world
- How to transition all those who are homeless to productive positions throughout society and the housing solutions that accompany that transition
- How to utilize and integrate the five God-given natural resources that can sustain humanity for eternity into our homes and communities—water, heat, light, air, and electricity—without having to pay for them
- How to generate power from only the local resources around the world
- How to generate pure water and grow food in all climates around the world
- How to provide individual and community sewer solutions around the world
- How to develop net zero communities with their own source of water, sewer, and electricity and not rely on city services or the electrical grid—totally sustainable

- Improve the indoor air quality, living conditions, and lower electricity costs by conducting a residential safety and energy retrofit to all existing homes worldwide and provide a zero-interest mortgage loan to fund the improvements
- Manufacture and distribute the best energy sources and storage options that are best suited for each region around the world
- Ultimately provide real solutions for ten of the seventeen Global Goals for Sustainable Development set out by the World Health Organization (WHO): no poverty, no hunger, good health, quality education, clean water and sanitation, renewable energy, good jobs, innovation and infrastructure, sustainable cities/communities, climate action
- Finally, bring together the complete team of the world's best professionals that can carry out and complete such an enormous task

The estimated cost for each of these endeavors is obviously unknown. The compounding benefits of vertical integration and direct sourcing will allow for a lower acquisition cost. The net zero aspect of each home will provide the lowest total cost of ownership that can be attained.

I began to receive a clear understanding of the big picture and the enormity of it all. It was a massive undertaking but something I felt comfortable with and quite capable of implementing. At the moment, the entire global plan is sixty-five pages in length and is capable of providing housing solutions for everyone on earth for the next one hundred plus years.

On the cover of the executive summary, I have written the following:

> For every house is built by someone, but
> God is the builder of Everything. (Hebrews 3:4)

The missions team at my church is currently operating on five continents. I've approached them and advised them that when the time is right, I want to assist them in providing sustainable housing for those in need worldwide. We will call it Kingdom Builders.

Looking back

Over those twenty-three years, I've experienced many seasons since then and am much more capable to receive that information today than I was twenty-three years ago. I am much more receptive and more attentive to what the Holy Spirit is doing in my life. I am much more experienced in the science of home building than I was back then.

In 2015, I was offered a job, unsolicited by the CEO of the country's largest energy rating firm, to show national home builders how to build according to the new energy codes. I was most fortunate to become a certified energy rater and learn the importance of how the science of a performing home can positively or negatively affect the occupants' health, safety, and their pocketbooks. All of this has seasoned me so that I have a more comprehensive understanding of what lies ahead and how to integrate those building principles into the Build His Kingdom plan.

The following verses encouraged me about the Holy Spirit revealing His plans:

> Commit to the Lord whatever you do, and He will establish your plans. (Proverbs 16:3 NIV)

> Call to me and I will answer you and tell you great and unsearchable things you do not know. (Jeremiah 33:3 NIV)

> He gave him the plans of all that the Spirit had put in his mind. (1 Chronicles 28:12 NIV)

> As for you, the anointing you received from him remains in you, and you do not need anyone to teach you. But as his anointing teaches you about all things and as that anointing is real, not counterfeit—just as it has taught you, remain in Him. (1 John 2:27 NIV)

> Strangers will shepherd your flocks; foreigners will work your fields and vineyards. (Isaiah 61:5 NIV)

> But store up for yourselves treasures in heaven, where moth and rust do not destroy, and where thieves do not break in and steal. (Matthew 6:20 NIV)

17

Confirmation of an Angel's Presence upon Request

Fast-forward to the spring of 2021, and I'm taking my four-mile walk every Monday, Wednesday, and Friday morning throughout the neighborhoods near my home. At that point, I had been walking the same route for about a year. When I walk, I pay very close attention to the sidewalk in front of me. I don't look around and stargaze. I have several friends that have cuts and bruises from tripping and falling during their morning walks.

During my hour-long morning walks, I sometimes listen to music on my headphones, and sometimes I spend that time in prayer. On this particular morning, I began to reflect over the years and noticed how the Holy Spirit had been "active" in my life. I distinctly remembered several circumstances where angels intervened and saved my life. I say angels because there is no other explanation that makes any sense. I had read my pastor's book on angels and confirmed that angels are there to guide us and protect us and help carry out the Lord's will in our lives. Also, in my pastor's book, he acknowledged that some angels do have wings. On this particular Wednesday morning, I was feeling a little brave and decided that if angels were real and they truly existed, I wanted to see real confirmation of their presence. As I walked, I began to pray, asking the Lord to show me proof that angels were present in my life. I didn't want to see evidence of past presence or anything else. I wanted to see real undeniable proof that angels were present in my life that day! I wanted to see a feather from an angel's wing. That is specifically what I prayed for. After about halfway around my four-mile circuit, I look down on the sidewalk, and this is what is in front of me:

Hmm. Please understand that I have been walking this same circuit for over one year three days a week, and I have *never* seen a feather on the sidewalk. This was the first time I had seen a feather, and it just so happened to be the only time I specifically prayed asking to see one. Coincidence, could be. Luck, I doubt it. It's typically quite windy where I walk, and the chances of a feather laying on an exposed sidewalk are extremely low.

I noticed something else that was different that day on my walk. I couldn't help but notice that robins were around me the entire time. As previously mentioned, I don't look around too often, but I am very aware of my surroundings. I began to notice that robins would repeatedly place themselves in the grass just off the sidewalk and hop along in front of me for a short distance. They would then flutter ahead of me until I caught up with them and continue to flutter along. It was not unusual to see two, three, or four robins at the same time along my path on that particular day. I didn't read anything into the presence of robins, but it did catch my attention, and I made a mental note of it.

Two days later on Friday morning, I had to eliminate any coincidence with the feather. So I prayed that the Holy Spirit would show me a white feather on my walk that day. Specifically, a fluffy white feather. Fluffy feathers are so light that they cannot sit still for one second on an exposed windy sidewalk. There was no way a fluffy white feather would be found on this particular day, but I threw it out there. I want to eliminate luck, coincidence, and anything else that might explain the existence of these feathers. I began to pray, and after reaching about three miles, I look down, and this is what I see:

It was a fluffy white feather sitting on top of the grass just off the edge of the sidewalk! I had chills running down me and couldn't help but feel overwhelmed at the sight of what was in front of me.

This really got my attention. Of course, I'd seen feathers before in various places, but those are very random occasions. The only two times in my sixty years that feathers appeared before me only after I prayed for them.

Interestingly enough, that very same day, I began to notice the robins again. They behaved in the same fashion that they did during my last walk day. They would appear just in front of me on either side of the sidewalk, then begin to hop and flutter along just ahead of me. They seemed to keep pace with me for a while then fly away. This time the number of robins increased. I counted twelve robins that day along my path. Just like the previous walk day, I noted how odd the robin sightings were and made another mental note. Honestly, I cannot explain the numerous robin sightings.

Over that weekend, I couldn't help but think about the answer to prayer that had occurred the last two days on my walk. There was still an ounce of doubt that had crept in, and I was feeling somewhat guilty about it. I still needed to know for sure that angels were present in my life. I still wanted to see more proof. I prayed and asked the Holy Spirit for one more feather. On that particular morning, I had business that I needed to deal with and decided that I would walk my four miles later that afternoon. That would give the wind plenty of time to blow away any lucky feathers laying around along my path. So about 5:00 p.m. that afternoon, I began my walk. I began to shamefully pray, asking the Holy Spirit to place a third feather in my path that day. Seeing one more feather on the third consecutive walk day would surely eliminate any doubt that I had of an angel's presence in my life. After about one mile, I looked down on the sidewalk, and this was in front of me:

One feather, then a second feather, and then a third feather all on the same walk day! Not only did I come upon a third feather on the third consecutive walk day but I came upon three separate feathers that day! Now that was amazing! I was now convinced that not only are angels real but they are present in my life. I had seen the evidence of their existence in other ways, but I had now experienced their presence only after specifically praying for it.

Again, the robins were back. This particular day, I counted sixteen robins that accompanied me along my walk. Clearly, something was going on. Was it the time of year? Was it the time of day? I certainly didn't pray on any of the three occasions to see robins! I still can't explain how I encountered well over thirty robins on three consecutive walk days.

I continued my morning walks after that day and searched and searched for feathers along my path without praying beforehand. I never saw any. Nor did I see any robins. Trust me when I say that I looked for them. I saw all kinds of other things along my walk, but I never saw feathers nor robins.

About a month and a half goes by, and one morning I randomly decide to pull a fast one and pray for undeniable, absolute, positive evidence of an angel's presence. I needed to see evidence one more time. I needed to see enough that I would know and not need to ask for evidence again. I did feel a little ashamed, and I felt like I was pushing it with God. I didn't want to make Him mad, but this sinner needed to know for sure. After walking about halfway around my circuit, I saw something very odd on the sidewalk in front of me. This is what I saw:

It was four feathers stuck to something on the sidewalk, arranged like a cross! This is the actual photo of what I saw that day. Not only were there four feathers but how they were arranged sent chills down my spine. I stopped walking and sat down on the sidewalk and wept. The robins were back too! Another sixteen robins encountered that day. Most definitely was not a coincidence!

I looked up and promised God that I would never ever doubt His nor His angels' presence in my life again! That was the undeniable proof that I needed. I walked the rest of the way home that day with a renewed faith that the Holy Spirit truly was with me and would gladly provide proof practically upon request.

It's now been a year since I saw those four feathers arranged like a cross on the sidewalk along with all the robins. I've continued to walk three days each week, and I never see feathers nor robins along my path. I no longer need to see feathers to know that the Lord and His angels are with me. I've been given all the proof that anyone should ever need. I do have a comfort and a peace about my spirit that I never had before. I feel more in tune with the Holy Spirit and much more attentive to my surroundings. I now know that angels are at work in my life, and I want to please the Lord as much as they do. I am extremely thankful for my renewed spirit and His presence!

Looking back

After plenty of time reflecting on past faith experiences over my lifetime, I came to the conclusion that the Lord was watching over me. There seemed to be too much evidence to deny it. What makes that even more significant is I'm a nobody. I'm just a normal guy living a normal life in a small town. I don't have a degree in theology, I'm not a pastor, nor am I a high-profile individual. I'm happy to say that I am a child of God made in His image and very blessed to be here.

So why me? I don't know the answer to that question. Here's what I do know. On a handful of days during my hourly walk, I was brave enough to ask to see proof that His angels were present in those moments on those given days. And I was given the proof! On the last occasion, I was almost ashamed to ask one last time to see proof because the continued evidence was overwhelmingly present.

As previously stated, I no longer seek proof that His angels are with me. I've been more than convinced. I cannot overstate how much that has inspired me and empowered me each and every day.

The following verses encouraged me about the Holy Spirit's presence:

> I will place a wool fleece on the threshing floor. If there is dew only on the fleece and all the ground is dry, then I'll know that you will save Israel by my hand, as you said. And that is what happened. Gideon rose early the next day; he squeezed the fleece and wrung out the dew—a bowlful of water. Then Gideon said to God, Do not be angry with me. Let me make just one more request. Allow me one more test with the fleece, but this time make the fleece dry and let the ground be covered with dew. That night God did so. Only the fleece was dry; all the ground was covered with dew. (Judges 6:37–40 NIV)

> He will cover you with his feathers, and under his wings you will find refuge; his faithfulness will be your shield and rampart. You will not fear the terror of night, nor the arrow that flies by day. (Psalm 91:4–5 NIV)

> He who loves Me will be loved by My Father, and I too will love him and show Myself to him. (John 14:21 NIV)

My Deepest Regret

When I look back during the days of losing all that weight, the key to my everyday success was getting on those scales every morning to receive the instant feedback from my efforts the day before. Whether the feedback was positive or negative, it allowed me the opportunity to manage each day in order to stay on course. Getting off course was bound to happen, but I was never off course more than one day.

Pilots set a compass heading and maintain constant feedback to ensure they stay on course. Ship captains do the same. Boy Scouts learn how to read a compass at an early age. Then how did I miss that one? How did I wander for over fifty years without checking my spiritual compass each day?

To sum it all up, my biggest regret in life is that I didn't seek the Lord on a daily basis when I was much younger. I didn't set aside a quiet time every day and read His word. I waited too long to get to know him intimately through prayer, meditation, and fasting. By not spending time with Him each day, I wandered off for months and years at a time. Consequently, I didn't develop an ear to hear His voice until much later in life. The same voice that told me to go build His kingdom. I can't help but think if I had put it all together when I was much younger, how much further down the road I would be in my walk with God. Sure, I read the Bible—from time to time. Sure, I prayed—periodically. I never meditated, nor did I ever fast until just a few years ago. I never put it all together on a daily basis. I missed out on the best part of life. If I had developed an ear to hear His voice earlier, just think of how many wrong turns in my life I could have avoided. All I had to do was seek Him daily and ask sooner!

That leads me to my only advice for my three sons and anyone who desires a blessed and enriched life. I can't write these words large enough, bold enough, or make them jump off the page enough. DON'T DO WHAT I DID! Please take this advice and benefit because God desires to know you.

So go and achieve the purpose for which God made you. That can't be done without seeking Him first with a whole heart. The way to seek Him is to set aside a daily time of prayer, meditation, and reading His word. Spend more time in prayer and fasting. Ask Him to guide you, protect you, speak to you so that His will can be carried out in your life. He absolutely will!

If I had only acted on the following verses sooner, my life would have been very different. They are my spiritual compass.

> For if you live according to the flesh, you will die; but if by the Spirit you put to death the misdeeds of the body, you will live. For those who are led by the Spirit of God are the children of God. (Romans 8:13–14)

> Each of you should use whatever gift you have received to serve others, as faithful stewards of God's grace in its various forms. If anyone speaks, they should do so as one who speaks the very words of God. If anyone serves, they should do so with the strength God provides, so that in all things God may be praised through Jesus Christ. (1 Peter 4:10–11 NIV)

> I urge you to live a life worthy of the call you have received. (Ephesians 4:1 NIV)

But you will receive power when the Holy Spirit comes on you; and you will be my witnesses in Jerusalem, and in all Judea and Samaria, and to the ends of the earth. (Acts 1:8 NIV)

Jesus states, "Therefore go and make disciples of all nations, baptizing them in the name of the Father, of the Son and of the Holy Spirit." (Matthew 28:1 NIV)

It Is My Hope

That my sons develop a deep relationship with the Lord so that when life's tragic events occur, they will be spiritually ready to lean on the Lord for comfort and understanding. If not, I know He will carry them.

That my unmarried sons going through tough times dating submit themselves to the Lord. Keep sticking to your faith, your core values, and your priorities while spending time with others. It's about friendship, genuine, heartfelt love, and compatibility because that is what lasts. Thirty-nine years together has proven that to be true in our lives.

That this single testimony will convince my sons and their families that the Lord's angels are very real and are ready to guard us, protect us, and rescue us in critical moments we find ourselves in.

That when my sons find themselves in a jobless situation or in a workplace transition, they will be encouraged. The Lord is in control and has the ability to overcome any challenge. Be open to what He brings you!

That each of my sons find their secular calling of serving the Lord.

That my sons are blessed to find themselves praying in a quiet place, reading His word, and hearing the voice of God speak to them. It will change their lives!

Our family can live with the faith that Habitat for Humanity demonstrates on a daily basis.

That by demonstrating how powerful prayer is even on seemingly trivial matters, I can use that example of finding my ancestor's grave to impact the lives of my sons and many generations beyond.

To be more in tune with my spirit so that I may know the angel's presence in various circumstances and experience those encounters on a deeper level.

To continue to surround myself with and seek other believers' advice on matters in my life. To continue to seek intercessors and hear from them on important events and decisions.

That family members who encounter one of God's angels is drawn closer to the Lord like I was. That event changed me and the course my life has taken. The Lord spoke through a half a dozen cardiologists to tell me that I was most fortunate to be alive and that He had a purpose for me.

That my sons and their families will understand where the source of their income is derived. I want so badly for them to experience the enriched lives that I know they will receive once they come to a place of obedience like Juli and I did. I pray that they won't wait until later in life to discover that blessing.

That I never wander away from the Lord again. I've paid the price for being lost. I'm humbled that my prayer was answered and the Lord showed me a path to healing my body. There's not a day that goes by that I don't thank Him for what He's doing in my life!

That after the tough times that I've endured, I am able to carry out my purpose for which God has placed me on this earth. I pray that I will hear Him when He speaks to me. I pray that He will use me as He made me to bring many souls into His kingdom.

That I will be blessed to witness the Lord's testimony more frequently. I very much want to experience His awesome timing and to see Him show himself in situations where He is undeniably exalted! It would be a wonderful day if the Lord would allow me to walk with Him like others have done in the past.

That I will be prepared to do my part when it comes time to build His kingdom. I pray that the Lord will guide my path and that He will protect us from those that are against us. I pray that He will use my skills to the fullest so we can bring millions of people to know Christ.

That someday I will meet my feathered angels face-to-face. I pray that all of my family members will be fortunate enough to have similar encounters with their angels as I did.

At the end of my life, I've fulfilled God's purpose that He had for me. I truly want to hear these words:

> Well done good and faithful servant! You have been faithful with a few things: I will put you in charge of many things. Come and share your master's happiness! (Matthew 25:21 NIV)

> Come, you who are blessed by the Father; take your inheritance, the kingdom prepared for you since the creation of the world. (Matthew 25:34 NIV)

I want everyone to hear these same words too! Go and seek the Lord, and ask Him to give you His special purpose and calling. Use that calling to lead others to know Christ. Then you can spend your life having the joy and peace of knowing that you have fulfilled your calling and purpose and that you will spend eternity in heaven with Jesus!

About the Author

Jeff grew up in what was a small town, Plano, Texas, and attended the First Christian Church. He developed a love of sports, especially baseball. He lettered both years as a starting first baseman for the Plano Wildcats. He later went to college at the University of Texas at Austin, pursuing a degree in business management.

He met the love of his life after college and married Juli in 1984. They have three wonderful sons—Brandon, Cameron, and Wesley. They still attend Prestonwood Baptist Church and love to spend their spare time in the Texas Hill Country.

A seventh-generation Texan, Jeff's family played a major role in placing early settlers in North Texas back in the early 1840s during the Republic of Texas days. A tradition he continues to this day. He's a fourth-generation Texas real estate licensee.

Also a fourth-generation home builder, Jeff grew up in a family of home builders and has built thousands of houses. Able to cut a roof at the age of fifteen, he spent his first twenty years building houses and working in senior management for national homebuilders across the US.

In 1993, he moved the family back to his hometown and made the transition to what would ultimately be his calling, selling real estate. Serving others as they transition in life fell in line with his technical knowledge of construction, his intimate knowledge of his hometown, and personal experiences of buying/selling homes as his family grew.

Jeff's real passion is hunting and fishing. After his grandfather took him under his wing as a young boy, he developed a love for the outdoors. Spending time in nature and watching the woods come alive as the sun arose each day were spiritual moments that shaped his childhood.

He and Juli enjoy traveling and taking their sons snow skiing and riding the fastest roller coasters they can find. Jeff especially enjoys hunting for rattlesnakes. Taking his sons rattlesnake hunting is still their best idea of an adrenaline rush. He greatly enjoys spending time with his family outdoors and has passed that love for the outdoors on to his sons.

Printed in the USA
CPSIA information can be obtained
at www.ICGtesting.com
LVHW052021180924
791308LV00020B/630